THE RAILWAY COMES TO DIDCOT

THE RAILWAY COMES TO DIDCOT

A HISTORY OF THE TOWN 1839 – 1918

BRIAN LINGHAM

ALAN SUTTON

First published in the United Kingdom in 1992 by
Alan Sutton Publishing Limited
Phoenix Mill · Far Thrupp · Stroud · Gloucestershire

First published in the United States of America in 1993 by
Alan Sutton Publishing Inc. · Wolfeboro Falls · NH 03896–0848

British Library Cataloguing in Publication Data
Lingham, B.F.
History of Didcot, 1841–1918
I. Title
942.579

ISBN 0-7509-0092-X

Library of Congress Cataloging in Publication Data applied for

For my mother, and sisters, Janet and Barbara, and
brother-in-law, Dave; and last, but not least,
Mrs Joan Simmons. Thank you all.

Typeset in 11/12 Sabon.
Typesetting and origination by
Alan Sutton Publishing Limited.
Printed in Great Britain by
The Bath Press, Avon.

Contents

Acknowledgements

I would like to acknowledge my debt to all those who have helped in my researches over the years, many of whom are now deceased, such as Mrs Grace Smith and Mr Walter Davies, who lived in Northbourne or Old Didcot respectively before the Great War. Also I am indebted to two people in particular, Mr Hector and Mrs Muriel Cullen of Newlands Avenue, who have answered my innumerable questions with good-humoured patience. Lastly, Martin and Mary Heard, who have done so much good work in Old Didcot recording and dating the period houses of the village and have always been ready with help and advice. Thank you all.

Introduction

In no way does this book, despite its title, pretend to be a history of the railway at Didcot. Such a history – the development of the junction and station, the layout of the tracks, types of engines used, the engine sheds and signal boxes, the broad gauge versus narrow gauge controversy – I leave to the specialist historian, such as Laurence Waters of Oxford. One of his books, *Didcot Junction and Railway Centre*, deals with the development of the station from 1844, and is heartily recommended. Other books which have been useful are McDermot's monumental three-volume work on the Great Western Railway and Paul Karau's history of the Didcot–Newbury–Southampton Railway.

The present book follows my earlier volume, *The Long Years of Obscurity* published in 1978, which covered the history of Didcot from the earliest times to the beginning of the period covered here.

My interest in the railway has been objective, and is limited to its influence on Didcot, and its future development and growth. Without the railway and its junction there would be no modern Didcot, just a small village the size of Appleford.

It was the army and its decision to site the arsenal and depot at Didcot that led to enlargement of the town during the 1930s. Again, it was its central position in the Great Western Railway system that led to the army selecting Didcot as the site of its depot.

1

The Railway Comes to Didcot, 1839–1862

No one today would argue with the premise that the growth of Didcot over the past 150 years is due to the railway, with some help from the army along the way: that this modern town with its urban sprawl of houses, schools, churches and road after road is, indirectly, the by-product of the Great Western Railway Company. But what is not generally appreciated is that it was not the siting of the station that gave the future town its growth – after all, Goring and Moulsford have stations, and they are still the villages that they were in 1839 – it was the creation of a junction at Didcot that made it such an important nodal point in the rail system, eventually giving access to all the main points of the compass. It was for this reason that the army decided to site its depot and arsenal here in 1915.

The story of Didcot and the railway really begins in 1833, at Bristol. During the 1820s and early '30s, Bristol, fearing that its port was in decline, especially in relation to Liverpool, its arch-rival commercially, and wanting a quick access to London for its goods, decided to have a survey made of a possible route for a railway line to the capital. A committee formed from the main commercial and other interests in the port appointed an engineer to undertake the survey – that engineer was Isambard Kingdom Brunel. He, with a colleague, set out immediately to survey two possible routes from Bristol to London: the first between Bath and Reading, via Bradford, the Pewsey Vale and Newbury; the second north of the Marlborough Downs, by Chippenham, Swindon, the Vale of the White Horse and the Thames Valley and then to Reading. Of the two, the second route was recommended. This way was preferred because of its easy gradients; those of the first route would have been too difficult for the primitive locomotives of the time, hence the detour north through the Vale of the White Horse and the Thames Valley.

The survey accepted by the committee, a company was formed, The Bristol and London Railroad, and then a second, influential committee was set up, this time in London. In August 1833, the two amalgamated to become the Great Western Railway Company. A prospectus was issued, and the route shown on the map included was, substantially, that which was afterwards laid down – the same as the line today. Didcot is not mentioned by name, but its position is indicated on the map as a likely junction for a 'probable branch' to Oxford.

A Bill was presented to parliament in 1834, which was approved only to be thrown out by the Lords. Although there was wide acceptance of the railway concept, an appreciation generally of the benefits such a system could bring to the country, equally there were strong objections from both vested interests and reactionary forces. These objections ranged from the Eton College Provost who feared that his boys might be corrupted if they had free access to London (and he was not mistaken); Windsor, which wanted the line routed nearer the town (Eton did not and managed to prevent it); Maidenhead, which also had its own fears, that there would be a loss in revenues from a decline in tolls paid to cross its bridge; farmers who feared competition from other farmers farther away from the capital; landowners generally who thought the value of their land might be affected by the railway; those with interests in road transport, the coach or wagon; and those who feared the use of canals and rivers would decline when competing with the railway. But these forces could not stand in the way of economic progress and were quickly swept aside. The Industrial Revolution could not function efficiently in the age of the horse: a new transport system was needed; the invention came at the right time and was quickly translated into reality by money and energy.

The Bill was resubmitted early 1835 and opponents, mainly now the London and Southampton Railway Company, and Eton (the other objectors having been appeased), could not gainsay the widespread support that had been whipped up the previous winter. The Bill then passed through both Houses, and received the Royal Assent 31 August 1835.

Work began shortly after the passing of the Bill at both the

London and the Bristol ends. Construction progressed steadily, and by June 1838 the London–Maidenhead section was ready for opening. At the beginning of 1839, the line was approaching the vicinity of Didcot. Contracts for the Didcot section, and immediately west for a distance of 14 miles, as far as Uffington, were issued in March. Later, in June, George Gibbs, one of the GWR's directors, came to Didcot where he 'met the clergy, farmers, road commissioners and lawyers of the neighbouring country and had a long talk with them about roads, drainage, bridges, etc., etc.'. In September, the *Reading Mercury* reported that

> between Twyford and Steventon the greater part of the line is already finished, and those works in course of execution are proceeding rapidly. The line is expected to open in the Spring. Although the embankment between Didcot and Steventon is the least advanced having been more recently commenced, construction is expected to be finished by Christmas.

It is not generally appreciated that the topography of Didcot was altered slightly; before the coming of the railway the land below and north of All Saints Church had sloped down gently to the meadows beyond. When the railway was laid down, a half-embankment was cut into and it destroyed the line of this slope. The original course of Lower Broadway–Abingdon Road was also altered (it was far more acute than it is today) when the line and Marsh Bridge were constructed.

The line was laid down and constructed by gangs of itinerant workers called navvies or navigators. They were a wild, lawless, violent breed of men, who were almost a law unto themselves. There were, it seems, about three hundred of them, encamped and working at or near Didcot during, probably, all of 1839 and early 1840. Newspapers of the times did report several incidents involving them. At Reading, they ran amuck after not being paid, and at Tilehurst there was an affray when a gang of them got drunk at the World's End Inn, with the publican's terrified wife and child left cowering inside the pub. There was a more serious incident at Hanney, this time almost a riot. Again, the *Reading Mercury* paints the scene. On 17 August

> the village of Hanney, near which the works of the GWR are in progress, was on Sunday, the scene of considerable disturbance

> and riot. It would appear that the navigators as the men are called had been very abusive to the villagers, who feeling greatly annoyed, mustered a stròng party and after some hard fighting, succeeded in ejecting them from the village. It was expected that the same would occur the following night but other than one or two skirmishes, nothing further occurred.

The Tame family, who have been a prominent farming family in this area for generations, recount one or two stories about local farmers against the navvies. Such as that concerning Edmund Tame, who was a 'perfect Samson'; he could lift up to 800 lbs in weight, bend half-crowns between his fingers, and tear up packs of cards. At that time – 1839 – the Tame farm was at East Hendred, its boundaries close to the railway line, which was still under construction. The navvies, just for devilment's sake, would let his cattle into the standing corn, which could be fatal, so they 'were spoiling for a fight'. They were only too aware of Edmund Tame, and wanted him to fight their champion, one Thompson. He was 6 ft 3 in and a veritable giant. Edmund was 6 ft 2 in; equally huge. The story continued,

> a ring was made and they fought four rounds, then Edmund got in a hammer blow on the navvie's head, and stunned him. He could not get up, and was out for six hours. Edmund was declared victor; the navvies cheering him from the ring. We never had any trouble from them again.

The Tames also recount that when Mr Edward Pullen was tenant at Foxhall Farm, in 1838, he too had a run in with the navvies. When they were digging out the cutting immediately to the west of the two Foxhall bridges, Mr Pullen caught them robbing his orchards. When he challenged them, they fired at him with dust shot. After they had gone, shot holes were found in the window shutters.

Quite obviously, they must have been a great nuisance to the villages along the line of construction, working as they did in large gangs, owing loyalty to their mates alone, almost like nomadic tribes. There was no one to control them; the contractors probably found it difficult, and possibly did not even try. There were no forces of law in existence at that time, at least not in the rural areas; just the annually elected village constable, who was only another villager serving his term, and was hardly trained or qualified to take on 300 navvies single-handed. They would have roamed the villages at the weekends,

GREAT WESTERN RAILWAY.

OPENING TO OXFORD.

On WEDNESDAY, the 12th of JUNE, 1844, the OXFORD RAILWAY will be opened for the Conveyance of PASSENGERS, Carriages, Horses, and Goods.

STATIONS AT DIDCOT JUNCTION, ABINGDON ROAD, AND APPLEFORD, WILL ALSO BE OPENED.

This Railway is now Completed to Exeter, Taunton, Bristol, Bath, &c.

EXETER is 45 miles from PLYMOUTH; CIRENCESTER is 15 miles from CHELTENHAM, 12 miles from STROUD, and 17 miles from GLOUCESTER.

HORSES and CARRIAGES being at those Stations, which are distinguished by Black Letter Type, ten minutes before the time specified for the departure of a Train, will be conveyed on this Railway. Horses only are conveyed to and from West Drayton.

The strong black marks or stops, under certain times of arrival shew, that the Trains do not proceed beyond the Stations on the same Line with them.

POST HORSES are kept in readiness at the principal Stations, and upon sufficient notice being given at Paddington, or at the Bull and Mouth Office, St. Martin's-le-Grand, would be sent to bring Carriages from any part of London to the Station, at a charge of 9s. west of St. Martin's Lane, and 10s. 6d. beyond it, both including Post Boy. Similar notice may be given at Bristol for Carriages to be brought from Clifton or the neighbourhood, to the Bristol Station.

TIME TABLE.

LONDON TIME is kept at all the Stations on the Railway, which is 4 minutes earlier than READING time; 5½ minutes before OXFORD time; 7½ minutes before CIRENCESTER time; 8 minutes before CHIPPENHAM time, 11 minutes before BATH and BRISTOL time; and 14 minutes before EXETER time. No Tickets will be issued after a Train is in sight at the intermediate Stations.

The Royal Hotel at Slough, and Railway Hotel at Reading, are open.

Distance	Down Trains.	DOWN TRAINS DAILY (excepting on Sundays).																		EVERY DAY 3rd Class Passengers and Goods.		TRAINS ON SUNDAYS ONLY.								
			Passengers & Goods.	DAY MAIL, Bristol to Exeter.				DAY MAIL to Bristol.											MAIL				Passengers & Goods.		DAY MAIL to Bristol.					MAIL
	Starting from	a.m.	a.m.	a.m.	a.m.	a.m.	a.m.	a.m.	a.m.	a.m.	noon.	p.m.	p.m.	p.m.	p.m.	p.m.	p.m.	p.m.	p.m.	a.m.	p.m.	a.m.	a.m.	a.m.	a.m.	a.m.	p.m.	p.m.	p.m.	p.m.
Mile	Paddington	..	..	..	6.0	..	8.0	9.0	1015	11.0	12.0	1.30	2.0	4.0	5.0	5.30	6.30	7.30	8.55	4.30	9.30	8.30	..	9.0	9.30	1015	2.0	5.0	7.0	8.55
5¼	Ealing	..	..	..	—	..	—	9.11	—	11.11	—	1.41	—	4.13	—	5.41	6.41	7.43	—	—	—	8.41	..	—	9.42	—	—	5.11	7.11	—
7¼	Hanwell	..	..	..	—	..	—	9.15	—	11.15	—	1.45	—	4.19	—	5.46	6.45	7.49	—	—	—	8.46	..	—	9.48	—	2.14	5.16	7.16	—
9	Southall	..	..	..	W	..	—	9.20	—	11.20	—	1.50	—	4.24	—	5.50	6.50	7.54	—	W	—	8.52	..	—	9.54	—	—	5.22	7.20	—
13	West Drayton	..	..	..	—	..	S	9.29	—	11.29	—	1.59	—	4.33	—	6.0	6.59	8.3	9.20	5.24	—	9.2	..	9.25	10.4	—	2.28	5.32	7.30	9.20
18	Slough	..	..	..	6.35	..	8.35	9.45	10.53	11.45	12.38	2.15	2.36	4.46	5.38	6.12	7.15	8.16	9.30	5.44	10.30	9.18	..	9.40	1020	10.52	2.40	5.45	7.42	9.30
22½	Maidenhead	..	..	..	6.45	..	8.48	9.55	11.3	1155	—	..	2.50	4.56	—	6.30	..	8.26	9.42	6.0	—	..	..	9.50	..	11.3	2.52	6.0	7.55	9.40
30¾	Twyford	..	..	..	—	..	9.5	..	—	..	1.8	..	3.8	5.12	6.3	..	..	8.42	—	—	11.14	..	..	10.10	..	—	3.10	..	8.12	—
35¾	Reading	..	..	..	7.10	..	9.18	..	11.35	..	1.20	..	3.22	5.25	6.17	..	..	8.55	10.10	7.20	11.40	..	..	1020	..	11.35	3.21	..	8.25	10.10
41½	Pangbourne	..	..	..	—	..	9.32	..	—	..	1.37	..	S	..	6.30	..	..	9.10	—	7.40	—	..	..	..	..	—	3.36	..	8.40	—
44¾	Goring	..	..	..	7.28	..	—	..	—	..	1.47	..	—	..	S	..	..	9.18	—	—	—	..	..	..	..	—	—	..	8.48	—
47¾	Wallingford Road	..	..	..	—	..	9.46	..	11.58	..	—	..	3.45	..	5.45	..	..	9.27	10.35	—	12.20	..	..	..	..	—	3.50	..	8.57	10.35
53	Didcot (Junction)	..	..	..	7.44	..	9.58	1115	12.12	..	2.6	..	3.58	..	6.58	..	..	9.40	10.48	8.20	1245	..	..	..	..	12.12	4.3	..	9.10	10.48
55	Appleford	..	..	..	—	..	10.10	—	—	..	2.14	..	—	..	—	..	..	9.50	—	10.10	..	..	..	..	..	..	4.11	..	9.20	..
56	Abingdon Rd.	..	..	..	7.55	..	10.13	—	12.23	..	2.17	..	4.10	..	7.10	..	..	9.53	11.0	10.13	..	..	..	..	..	12.23	4.15	..	9.23	11.0
63	Oxford	..	..	..	8.10	..	1030	11 36	1238	..	2.35	..	4.25	..	7.25	..	..	1010	11.13	1030	..	..	..	..	..	1238	4.30	..	9.40	11 16
56¼	Steventon	..	..	..	7.50	..	—	..	—	..	2.17	..	—	..	7.8	..	..	..	—	—	..	..	..	..	..	..	4.1	..	..	..
63¼	Faringdon Road	..	..	..	8.7	..	—	..	12.38	..	2.32	..	4.23	..	7.23	..	..	..	11.12	—	1.19	..	..	..	..	12.38	4.33	..	..	11.12
71¼	Shrivenham	..	..	..	—	..	10.40	..	—	..	2.50	..	4.41	..	7.40	..	..	..	—	9.30	—	..	..	..	..	—	4.45	..	..	—
77	Swindon (Junct.)	..	..	..	8.40	..	10.55	..	1.5	..	3.5	..	4.55	..	7.50	..	..	..	11.40	10.0	2.15	..	..	..	..	1.5	5.0	..	..	11.4
	Dep. for Cheltenham	..	..	..	9.2	..	11.7	..	1.17	..	3.17	..	5.7	..	8.2	..	..	..	11.52	11.7	9.2	..	..	..	..	1.17	5.12	..	..	11.52
81½	Purton	..	..	..	9.10	..	—	..	1.27	..	—	..	5.17	..	—	..	..	..	—	—	9.10	..	..	..	..	1.27	5.20	..	..	—
85½	Minety	..	..	..	9.20	..	11.23	..	1.38	..	3.32	..	5.27	..	8.22	..	..	..	—	11.23	9.20	..	..	..	..	1.38	5.30	..	..	—
95	Cirencester	..	..	..	9.50	..	1150	..	2.5	..	4.5	..	5.53	..	8.50	..	..	..	1235	11 50	9.50	..	..	..	a.m.	2.5	5.55	..	..	1235
—	Swindon, Jun. (Dep.)	..	..	..	8.50	..	11.5	..	1.15	..	3.15	..	5.5	..	8.0	..	..	..	11.50	11.10	2.30	..	..	..	8.45	1.15	5.10	..	..	11.50
82¾	Wootton Basset	..	..	..	9.3	..	—	..	—	..	3.27	..	5.18	..	8.12	..	..	..	—	11.40	—	..	..	..	8.57	—	5.22	..	..	—
93¾	Chippenham	..	..	..	9.28	..	11.35	..	1.45	..	3.50	..	5.40	..	8.33	..	..	..	12.20	12.30	3.45	..	..	..	9.22	1.45	5.45	..	..	12.20
98¾	Corsham	Passengers & Goods	..	..	9.38	..	11.47	..	—	..	4.2	..	—	..	8.43	..	..	..	—	—	—	..	..	..	9.33	—	5.55	..	..	—
101¾	Box		..	a.m.	9.48	a.m.	11.57	p.m.	—	..	—	p.m.	6.0	..	8.52	..	p.m.	..	—	—	—	..	..	a.m.	9.43	—	6.7	..	p.m.	—
106¾	Bath	4.30	..	8.40	10.0	11.0	12.10	1.0	2.10	..	4.20	5.30	6.15	..	9.10	..	9.30	..	12.50	1.10	4.30	..	..	8.40	9.55	2.10	6.18	..	9.30	12.50
108¾	Twerton	..	..	8.45	—	11.5	—	1.5	—	..	—	5.35	—	..	—	..	9.35	..	—	—	—	..	..	8.45	—	2.15	—	..	9.34	—
111¾	Saltford	..	..	8.53	—	11.13	—	1.13	—	..	—	5.45	—	..	—	..	9.42	..	—	—	—	..	..	8.53	—	—	—	..	9.42	—
113¾	Keynsham	..	..	9.0	10.20	11.20	—	1.20	—	..	4.35	5.50	—	..	—	..	9.49	..	—	—	—	..	..	9.0	10.15	2.25	6.40	..	9.48	—
118¼	Bristol { arrival	5.20	a.m.	9.10	10.30	11.30	12.35	1.30	2.35	..	4.50	6.0	6.40	..	9.40	..	10.0	..	1.15	1.45	5.20 a.m.	..	a.m.	9.10	1025	2.35	6.48	..	10.0	1.15
	Bristol { departure	..	7.0	9.20	10.50	..	12.50	..	2.45	..	5.5	..	6.55	..	..	..	..	..	1.25	..	7.0	..	7.0	9.20	..	2.55	7.5	..	..	1.25
126¼	Nailsea	..	—	9.38	—	..	1.8	..	—	..	5.23	..	7.13	..	..	..	..	..	—	..	—	..	—	9.38	..	—	7.23	..	..	—
130¼	Clevedon Rd. Yattn.	..	7.45	9.48	11.18	..	1.18	..	3.8	..	5.34	..	7.23	..	..	..	..	..	—	..	7.45	..	7.45	9.48	..	3.20	7.32	..	..	—
133¾	Banwell [Junc.	..	7.56	—	11.25	..	—	..	—	..	5.43	..	—	..	..	..	..	..	—	..	7.58	..	7.56	9.55	..	—	7.40	..	..	—
136¾	Weston Super Mare	..	8.10	10.5	11.35	..	1.28	..	3.23	..	5.50	..	7.40	..	..	..	..	..	—	..	8.10	..	8.10	10.0	..	3.35	7.49	..	..	—
145¼	Highbdge. nr. Burnham	..	8.42	10.23	11.53	..	—	..	3.41	..	6.10	..	7.58	..	..	..	..	..	—	..	8.42	..	8.42	10.24	..	3.53	8.7	..	..	—
151¼	Bridgewater	a.m.	9.5	10.40	12.10	..	2.0	..	3.55	..	6.25	..	8.15	..	..	..	..	..	2.35	..	9.5	a.m.	9.5	10.40	..	4.10	8.24	..	..	2.35
163	Taunton	8.0	9.50	11.0	12.30	..	2.25	..	4.15	..	6.50	..	8.35	..	..	..	..	..	3.0	..	9.50	8.0	9.50	11.0	..	4.30	8.45	..	..	3.0
170	Wellington	8.15	10.15	11.15	12.45	..	—	..	4.30	..	7.5	..	8.50	..	..	..	..	..	3.15	..	10.35	8.15	10.35	11.15	..	4.45	9.0	..	..	3.15
179	Tiverton Road	8.34	11.10	11.35	1.10	..	2.55	..	4.50	..	7.30	..	9.15	..	..	..	..	..	3.35	..	11.10	8.30	11.10	11.35	..	5.5	9.25	..	..	3.35
181¼	Collumpton	8.39	..	11.40	1.17	..	3.0	..	—	..	7.37	..	9.22	..	..	..	..	..	3.40	..	11.45	8.35	..	11.40	..	5.10	9.32	..	..	3.40
185¼	Hele	8.49	..	11.48	1.27	..	3.10	..	5.3	..	7.47	..	9.32	..	..	..	..	..	—	..	12.5	8.45	..	11.48	..	5.20	9.42	..	..	—
193¾	Exeter	9.0	..	12.5	1.45	..	3.30	..	5.20	..	8.5	..	9.50	..	..	..	..	..	4.5	..	1235	9.0	..	12.5	..	5.35	10.0	..	..	4.5

Distance	Up Trains.	UP TRAINS DAILY, (excepting on Sundays.)																	EVERY DAY 3rd Class Passengers and Goods.		TRAINS ON SUNDAYS ONLY.									
							DAY MAIL from Bristol.						DAY MAIL from Exeter.		Passengers & Goods.			MAIL				DAY MAIL Bristol to London.			DAY MAIL from Exeter.		Passengers & Goods.			MAIL
	Starting from	a.m.	a.m.	a.m.	a.m.	a.m.	a.m.	a.m.	a.m.	a.m.	a.m.	p.m.	p.m.	p.m.	p.m.	p.m.	p.m.	p.m.	p.m.	p.m.	a.m.	a.m.	a.m.	p.m.	p.m.	p.m.	p.m.	p.m.	p.m.	p.m.
Miles	Exeter	..	..	..	..	..	..	7.0	8.30	9.15	1030	..	1246	..	2.0	3.15	5.15	9.35	..	2.0	7.0	9.15	..	..	..	1246	..	2.0	5.15	9.35
8¼	Hele	..	..	..	..	..	..	7.17	8.45	9.32	—	..	1.0	..	2.25	3.31	5.33	—	..	2.25	7.17	9.32	..	..	..	1.0	..	2.25	5.33	—
12¼	Collumpton	..	..	..	..	..	..	7.25	8.54	9.42	10.53	..	1.8	..	2.45	3.39	5.42	9.57	..	2.45	7.25	9.42	..	..	..	1.8	..	2.45	5.42	9.57
14¾	Tiverton Road	..	..	..	..	..	..	7.30	8.59	9.48	10.58	..	1.12	..	3.0	3.44	5.45	10.1	..	3.0	7.30	9.48	..	..	..	1.12	..	3.0	5.48	10.1
23¾	Wellington	..	..	..	..	..	..	7.50	9.18	1010	11.18	..	1.34	..	3.45	4.3	6.10	10.23	..	3.45	7.50	1010	..	..	..	1.31	..	3.45	6.10	10.23
30¾	Taunton	..	..	..	..	..	..	8.5	9.32	..	11.32	..	1.47	..	4.25	4.17	6.30	10.40	..	4.25	8.5	..	..	..	..	1.47	..	4.25	6.30	10.40
42¾	Bridgewater	..	..	..	..	..	..	8.30	9.52	For Down Trains only.	11.53	..	2.7	..	5.10	4.37	6.55	11.5	..	5.10	8.30	..	..	..	..	2.7	..	5.10	6.55	11.5
48¾	Highbridge	..	..	..	..	..	..	8.45	10.5		—	..	2.19	..	5.45	4.50	7.10	—	..	5.45	8.45	..	..	..	..	2.19	..	5.45	7.19	—
	Starting from																													
58¾	W. S. Mare Station	..	..	..	..	..	..	8.35	9.55	11 25	12.5	..	2.23	..	5.0	5.0	7.20	—	..	5.0	8.35	..	..	..	..	2.23	..	5.0	7.20	—
60	Banwell	..	..	..	..	..	..	9.12	—	—	12.29	..	—	..	—	—	7.37	—	..	—	9.12	..	..	..	..	—	..	—	7.37	—
63¾	Clevedon R. Yattn	..	..	..	..	..	..	9.21	10.35	—	12.36	..	2.51	..	6.45	5.20	7.46	—	..	6.45	9.21	..	..	..	..	2.51	..	6.45	7.46	—
67¾	Nailsea	..	..	..	..	..	..	9.31	—	—	12.45	..	—	..	—	5.30	7.56	—	..	—	9.31	..	..	..	..	3.0	..	—	7.56	—
75¼	Bristol { arrival	..	..	..	a.m.	a.m.	a.m.	9.50	11.5	noon.	1.5	..	3.25	p.m.	7.30	5.50	8.15	12.15	..	7.30	9.50	..	a.m.	..	..	3.25	p.m.	7.30	8.15	12.15
	Bristol { departure	..	..	..	7.0	8.0	8.35	10.0	11.15	12.0	1.15	..	3.40	4.30	10.0	6.0	8.30	12.25	2.30	10.0	..	8.0	8.35	..	..	3.40	6.30	..	8.30	12.25
80¼	Keynsham	..	..	..	—	8.10	—	10.10	11.25	12.10	—	..	3.50	4.40	—	—	8.40	—	—	—	..	8.10	—	..	..	3.50	6.40	..	8.40	—
82¼	Saltford	..	..	..	—	—	—	10.16	—	12.16	—	..	—	4.46	—	—	8.46	—	—	—	..	8.16	—	..	..	—	6.46	..	8.46	—
85¼	Twerton	..	..	..	—	8.18	—	10.22	—	12.22	—	..	—	4.52	—	—	8.52	—	—	—	..	8.22	—	..	..	—	6.52	..	8.52	—
87	Bath	..	..	..	7.25	8.25	9.0	1030	11.43	1230	1.40	..	4.7	5.0	1045	6.25	9.0	12.45	3.15	10.45	..	8.30	9.0	..	..	4.10	7.0	..	9.0	12.45
92	Box	..	..	..	7.36	..	—	..	11.55	..	1.55	..	4.20	..	..	6.37	..	—	—	—	..	..	9.13	..	..	4.21	7.12	..	..	—
95¾	Corsham	..	..	..	—	..	9.23	..	12.7	..	2.5	..	4.32	..	..	6.50	..	—	—	—	..	..	9.23	..	..	4.35	7.26	..	..	—
100	Chippenham	..	..	..	8.2	..	9.35	..	12.20	..	2.17	..	4.44	..	..	7.2	..	1.15	4.5	11.30	..	..	9.35	..	..	4.47	7.40	..	..	1.15
111	Wootton Basset	..	..	..	—	..	9.59	..	12.45	..	—	..	5.8	..	..	—	..	—	4.45	—	..	..	9.59	..	..	5.10	8.0	..	..	—
	Starting from																													
124¾	Cirencester	..	..	..	7.50	..	9.25	..	1215	..	1.45	..	4.10	..	..	6.45	..	1.5	4.10	1.5	..	..	9.25	..	..	4.10	—	..	..	1.5
125	Minety	..	..	..	8.15	..	—	..	12.37	..	2.10	..	4.38	..	..	7.10	..	—	4.38	—	..	..	9.51	..	..	4.38	—	..	..	—
121	Purton	..	..	..	8.23	..	10.0	..	—	..	2.20	..	4.50	..	..	7.20	..	—	4.50	—	..	..	10.5	..	..	4.50	—	..	..	—
116¾	Swindon Junction { Arrival	..	..	..	8.37	..	10.13	..	1.0	..	2.45	..	5.20	..	..	7.30	..	1.50	5.5	1.50	..	..	10.13	..	..	5.25	8.10	..	..	1.50
	Swindon Junction { Departure	..	..	..	8.47	..	10.23	..	1.10	..	2.55	..	5.30	..	..	7.40	..	2.0	5.40	2.20	..	..	10.23	..	..	5.35	..	..	..	2.0
122¾	Shrivenham	..	..	..	8.58	..	10.35	..	1.23	..	—	..	5.42	..	..	—	..	—	6.5	—	..	..	10.35	..	..	5.49	..	..	..	—
130	Faringdon Road	..	..	..	9.13	..	10.50	For Down Day Mail	—	..	3.20	..	—	..	..	8.8	..	2.25	6.35	—	..	..	10.50	..	..	6.5	..	..	..	2.25
137¼	Steventon	..	..	..	9.28	..	—		—	..	—	..	6.10	..	..	—	..	—	7.15	—	..	..	—	..	..	6.19	..	..	..	—
	Starting from			a.m.																										
150¼	Oxford	..	..	7.50	9.10	..	1045	11 45	1.35	..	3.15	..	5.45	..	..	8.0	..	2.20	5.45	2.20	..	7.20	1045	..	..	3.50	..	..	..	2.20
143¼	Abingdon Rd.	..	..	8.5	9.25	..	11.0	11.58	1.50	..	3.30	..	6.5	..	..	8.15	..	2.35	6.5	2.35	..	7.35	11.0	..	..	6.10	..	..	..	2.35
142¾	Appleford	..	..	8.8	—	..	—	—	1.53	..	—	..	6.10	..	..	—	..	—	6.10	—	..	7.38	—	..	..	6.15	..	..	..	—
140¼	Didcot	..	..	[illegible]	[illegible]	..	11.10	1210	2.0	..	3.40	..	6.16	..	..	8.28	..	2.49	7.30	4.0	..	7.4	11.10	..	..	6.25	..	..	..	[illegible]
146½	Wallingford R.	..	..	8.30	—	..	11.28	..	2.20	..	—	..	6.33	..	..	—	..	3.6	7.45	—	..	[illegible]	11.28	..	..	6.42	..	..	..	[illegible]
149½	Goring	..	..	8.38	9.55	..	—	..	—	..	—	..	6.40	..	..	—	..	—	—	—	..	[illegible]	—	..	..	—	..	..	..	—
152½	Pangbourne	a.m.	..	8.46	10.2	..	11.40	..	—	..	4.10	..	—	..	..	8.54	..	—	8.10	—	..	8.16	11.40	..	..	6.55	..	a.m.	..	—
158	Reading	7.30	..	9.0	10.16	..	11.53	..	2.42	..	4.25	..	6.58	..	..	9.8	..	3.30	9.20	5.0	..	8.30	11.53	..	..	7.7	..	9.0	..	[illegible]
163	Twyford	7.40	..	9.10	10.26	a.m.	—	[illegible]	55	..	—	..	7.10	p.m.	..	9.20	..	—	10.5	—	..	8.4	—	..	p.m.	7.20	..	[illegible]	..	
171¾	Maidenhead	7.55	a.m.	9.30	10.40	1115	12.20	1.45	—	..	4.52	p.m.	7.27	8.30	..	9.37	..	4.0	—	6.0	a.m.	9.0	12.20	p.m.	6 30	[illegible]	..	9.27	..	[illegible]
175¾	Slough	8.6	9.0	9.10	10.50	11.25	12.30	2.0	3.25	..	5.5	6.0	7.37	8.45	..	9.47	..	4.10	10.45	6.30	8.0	9.10	12.30	5.0	6.45	7.50	..	[illegible]	..	[illegible]
180¼	West Drayton	8.18	9.10	9.53	—	11.37	—	2.10	—	..	—	6.10	—	8.55	..	—	..	4.22	—	6.50	8.10	[illegible]	—	5.12	6.57	—	..	[illegible]	..	..
184¾	Southall	8.28	9.19	10.3	—	11.46	—	2.19	—	..	—	6.19	—	9.5	..	—	..	—	T.	—	8.19	[illegible]	—	5.21	7.5	—	..	[illegible]	..	..
186¾	Hanwell	8.33	9.24	10.9	—	11.51	—	2.24	—	..	—	6.24	—	9.10	..	—	..	—	—	—	8.24	[illegible]	—	5.27	7.15	—	..	..	..	..
188¾	Ealing	8.38	9.28	10.14	—	11.56	—	2.28	—	..	—	6.28	—	9.15	..	—	..	—	—	—	8.28	9.41	—	5.32	7.18	—	..	10.16	..	—
193¾	Paddington	8.55	9.45	1020	11.30	1215	1.10	2.45	4.10	..	5.30	6.45	8.20	9.30	..	1030	..	4.50	12.0	7.45	3.45	10.0	1.10	5.50	7.30	8.35	..	1030	..	4.50

N. B.—Trains will stop on particular days as indicated by the letters, T Tuesday—W Wednesday—S Saturday.

N. B.—The Time Table is calculated throughout at London Time.

Children under two years of age travel "free;" and those under 10 years of age at half-price.

17 June, 1844. J. T. NORRIS, PRINTER, ALDERSGATE STREET. **Turn over.**

This timetable was issued for the opening of the Oxford Railway on 12 June 1844. *(Laurence Waters)*

especially if there was a pub, terrorizing, stealing, drunkenly violent. It must have been like this at Didcot – and it lasted for over a year. Their camp was obviously sited near or by the line of construction, and equally near to the village. At Hanney, as the newspaper reported, the villagers had had enough, and solved their own problem by fighting to get rid of them. This report was just the tip of the iceberg; and there must have been many such incidents like this, unknown and unrecorded.

To construct the railway through Didcot, the company needed to acquire a strip of land. This was purchased in five blocks, and measured just over 19 acres. The landowners from whom this land was acquired were Colonel John Blagrave, the Revd R.P. Morrell, William Taylor and the Revd R.D. Murray. The land that William Taylor sold was glebe land (he was the Rector's tenant), which he did on behalf of the Rector, the Revd R. Nicholson. Brasenose College, who were owners of the living, to which they had presented the Revd Nicholson, also acted on his behalf as agents, being paid £1,100 for the land. This part of the glebe was roughly the strip of land on which the railway now runs from the station to the western border of Didcot. It, together with Col. Blagrave's land, formed the two largest blocks. The station and its forecourt were built on the colonel's land.

The great day arrived; and the latest part of the railway newly completed stretching from Reading to Steventon, with intermediate stations at Pangbourne, Goring and Moulsford, opened 1 June 1840. There was pandemonium that day as thousands converged on Steventon; as *Jackson's Oxford Journal* reported on the 6th

> [the] journey from London takes 1hr 10 minutes; an incredible time! thousands of spectators flocked to Steventon, normally a quiet village, was overwhelmed. In the afternoon the first train arrived, 'The Leopard'. Many people, just for curiosity's sake went to an thro to London and back again.

The *Reading Mercury* reported that every road in the direction of Steventon was crowded with pedestrians and wheeled vehicles of every kind. The *Charon* brought the directors of the GWR down from London. It was so successful that it was reported that the receipts for the first week were £5,503. Obviously, every train was crowded with sightseers, although fares, even by the standard of the times, were not cheap: 12*s.* 6*d.* (62½p) 1st class, and 8*s.* 6*d.*

(42½p), 2nd class. It was not long before coach operators were setting up services to meet trains at Steventon and at Cholsey and Moulsford. Some coaches were even coming from as far away as Birmingham. The newspapers carried many advertisements for coach services to stations at Faringdon Road (Challow), Steventon, Cholsey and Moulsford. Coaches were still travelling to London, to be used by those who distrusted or were afraid of the railway. An advert appeared in May 1842, for the *Prince of Wales*, a stagecoach travelling from Oxford to London, via High Wycombe, to the Bull Inn, Holborn, taking five and a half hours, at a cost of inside 12*s*., outside 6*s*. The traffic to Steventon was so great with coaches meeting every train – eight a day – that the Turnpike Trustees for the Abindon–Newbury turnpike soon set up new toll gates, and, presumably, at both ends of the village.

It is really impossible for us to appreciate the effect the railway had on the lives of people at the time; indeed, *Jackson's Oxford Journal* did actually comment that the 'effect on North Berkshire has been very great'. The amazement felt by the *Journal*'s correspondent when he observed the opening of the railway on 1 June is still very apparent even after 150 years. He did find it incredible.

In September 1840, a comparison was made in the same newspaper of relative times for coach and train, both travelling to London, that showed how journey times had been transformed. In 1813, a coach travelling from Cheltenham, with an overnight stop at Oxford, took thirty hours. The train time Bristol–London was six hours. While sending goods from Bristol to London by road, canal and river (if not in flood) could at best take up to three days, the train time was again six hours. Life was truly transformed and would never be the same again.

Steventon continued for the next four years to be the main junction for the area: where passengers disembarked for Oxford and other destinations, catching one of the many coaches waiting outside the station. In 1842, over 77,000 passengers and 12,500 tons of goods were transported via Steventon.

Steventon's reign of supremacy lasted for just four short years, for on 12 June 1844, Didcot Junction and Station were opened, and so too was the branch to Oxford.

The Oxford branch was long in the winning. The GWR had to contend with intractable objections from both Oxford University and the people of Abingdon. Proposals for the Oxford branch had been put forward by the GWR in 1837, 1838 and in 1840, and each

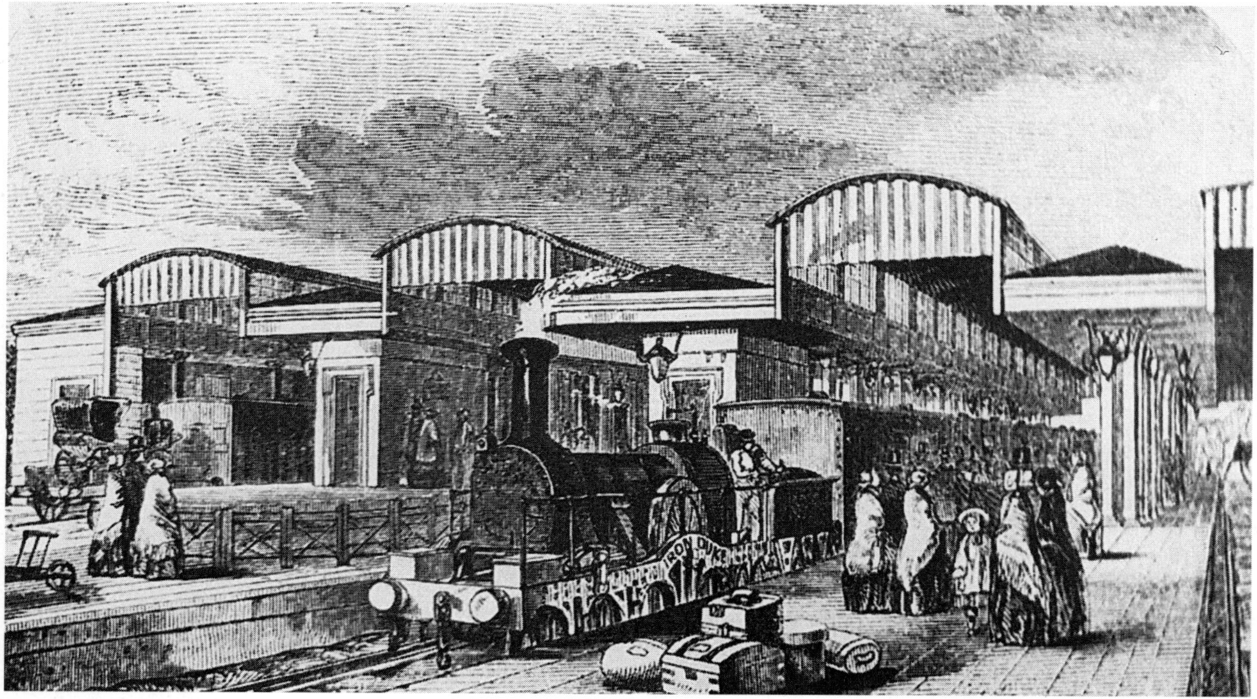

Brunel's original station of 1844, shown looking west in 1852. This line drawing is the only view that still exists. The station was rebuilt in the early 1880s in response to increasing traffic.

time they were opposed successfully. The first Bill of 1837, which laid out a line running from Didcot and Oxford, with a terminus near Magdalen Bridge, included a spur to Abingdon. With Oxford pacified by extra clauses in the Bill, it passed the Lower House, only to be thrown out by the Lords, due to the opposition of two local landowners, who owned 4½ miles of the projected route of 9 miles. They felt that the railway would ruin the land – a commonly held objection. The Bill was revived again the next year, only to be rejected, due this time to both the opposition of Abingdon's MP (even though the company had left the spur to that town out of the Bill) and the university, whose Chancellor, the Duke of Wellington had led the fight. He felt that the railways would 'encourage the lower classes to move about'. Another attempt in 1840 was also defeated. So for the next four years Steventon remained Oxford's link to the railway, with its eight coaches a day. The two-hour journey cost 3*s*.

Most of the standard histories tend to concentrate mainly on the opposition of Oxford to the railway Bills, while that of Abingdon is given less prominence. Oxford's objections were that the existing links with London were more than adequate, that the railway would lead to poor discipline at the university, and that construction would cause flooding. However, there was some opposition in the town to the university's views, with strong conflict in attitudes.

It is quite curious today that there is a strong belief widely held both at Abingdon, and locally, at Didcot, for instance, that had it not been for the intransigence of the burghers of the town the railway would have gone to Abingdon, through and then on to Swindon. Or, alternatively, the Oxford branch had been intended to go through the town on its way to the city. All untrue. There was never any intention on the part of the GWR to take the line anywhere near Abingdon – the nearest it would get would be 4 miles away, but linked by the spur. The main line of today, and the Oxford branch, both follow the route as surveyed and laid down by Brunel and the company between 1839 and 1844; and from the beginning, the line to Oxford was meant to break off at Didcot. This is shown clearly in the map of 1833. The 1837 Bill did include the spur, but opposition caused it to be dropped; and it was not included in subsequent Bills. Opposition from Abingdon was total from the start; neither the railway nor its spur was wanted anywhere near the town. Many meetings were held in Abingdon against the GWR and its various Bills: the townspeople felt that injury would result to river embankments from the erection of bridges and must considerably deteriorate the value of property;

there would be a loss of land and damage to roads; the projected line of the railway from Oxford to Didcot was unnecessary and uncalled for; and that there would be heavy traffic coming to and through the town. These attitudes remained fairly constant until about 1843, when cracks appeared and shifts in opinions in favour of the GWR took place. But it was too late; the line was under construction. Abingdon had to wait until 1856, when it was finally connected to the Oxford–Didcot line by its own branch. However, despite all these objections, on the fourth attempt the Didcot–Oxford Bill passed both Houses, and received the Royal Assent, 11 April 1843.

Owing to some difficulties, work did not begin until October, but proceeded rapidly due to a mild winter. Again there were problems with the navvies; the newspapers reported several incidents. The line was completed quickly. The branch line, with Didcot Junction and Station, was opened 12 June 1844. The new junction was a large station, consisting of four lines and five very narrow platforms, which were covered by a single overall roof completely made of wood and designed by Brunel. Until quite recently, it was thought that this station had been burnt down in the great fire of 1886, but modern research has shown that the station had been extensively remodelled during the years 1882 and 1885.

Didcot rather than Steventon was selected as the site for the new junction because it was low lying; it was also level, and so too was the rest of the land through to Oxford. It presented no major engineering problems, other than the construction of two wooden trestle bridges which carried the line across the Thames. Gradients were very important in those early days: that is why Steventon, a seemingly perfect choice for the junction, was never considered, because of its position on the side of a hill, and the fact that any track would have to skirt Boars Hill. It was impossible for early locomotives to climb even slight gradients pulling coaches. If one looks at the course of the line through Didcot, it can be seen clearly that every effort has been made to keep the line level, with embankments at one end and cuttings at the other.

The station established, it was at least a year before the development of its forecourt began. Presumably, the roundabout arrangement that had existed before the western half of Station Road was built in 1917 had been laid out when the station was built; and the mound (which was still there until quite recently) was probably made up of the earth dug when the station tunnels were constructed.

In 1846, the Junction Hotel and Tavern (or the Tap) was opened;

The Great Western Junction Hotel, opened in 1846 and photographed by Henry Taunt in c. *1905.* *(Don Farnborough)*

this was the first of the hotels to be built. The builder was, possibly, John Blagrave – he certainly owned the land on which the hotel now stands. He had also been the previous owner of the station site and all the land that had surrounded it.

During those immediate years, just after the opening of the junction, there were three possible routes to the station: up Foxhall Road to the bridge, then down the footpath beside the line, or through the village, and then to the station. The other route may well have been up what was then known as 'Long Strings Lane' (now Britwell Road), down Lydalls Road and along to the station.

This situation lasted until 1847; it was then that the GWR laid down Station Road. The company needing an outlet to the main road, purchased from the Revd William Baker, then lord of the manor and owner of Manor Farm, a strip of land that ran from the station up to the highway. This road, known then as the Wallingford Road (and now the Broadway) was, before 1879, part of a turnpike road – the Wallingford–Faringdon Turnpike Road. With the large increase in traffic to the new station, the trustees responded by opening two new gates. The first in 1846, near the Park Road–Foxhall Road junction, and known as the Didcot

The Old White Hart, built in 1846, and photographed just before its demolition in 1927.

Gate, the second, in *c.* 1859, at the Hagbourne Road junction.

(Another building of the period was the old White Hart, which stood formerly at the top of Station Road (it was replaced in 1927 by the present public house). It is somewhat difficult to establish exactly when it was built because New House (demolished in 1960; its site is now a petrol station), at the bottom of Foxhall Road, was also at that time trading as an inn, and known too as the White Hart. This house, as part of the Manor Farm estates, was described as an inn when sold in 1857 by the Revd Baker to Lord Overstone.

But it does seem likely that the new White Hart was built in 1846, and soon afterwards the former inn reverted to what it had been formerly, a farmhouse. The new inn was in a perfect position, at the junction of the new road with the turnpike. What better position to entice passing traffic or that going down to the new station. It does seem to have been the local for those early railwaymen. The publicans during this period were William Dunsden at the old White Hart, and at the new, Edmund Miles. The new inn was built and owned by the H. & C. Simmonds Brewery.

As can be imagined, there was a tremendous flood of new people into Didcot, all seeking accommodation for themselves and their families, and finding nothing – what was available was quickly snapped up. Little was done by the GWR to alleviate this demand. However, it does seem that they were indirectly responsible for erecting a terrace of ten cottages which stood formerly at the top of Station Road, called Mount Pleasant but known as 'The Barracks' by locals. These were built in 1852 by a James Ploughman. Other terrace blocks were built in the village, in response to the same demands, and from the same workers.

After the building of Junction Hotel, there was no further development of the station forecourt until the opening of the Didcot Corn Exchange in 1857. The prime movers in its opening, which had taken five years to reach fruition, were W.J. Williams of Harwell and Richard Belcher of Blewbury. *Jackson's Oxford Journal* reported that

> they continued agitating the subject until at last they rallied around them a sufficient number of persons who thought, with them, that it was an undertaking which could not fail to succeed, and be a benefit to the surrounding district.

The company was formed and its Board of Directors were William Hayward, of Wittenham (Chairman), Messrs J. Louseley of Appleford, Collen, Fisher and R. Belcher, and W.J. Williams (Secretary).

The GWR, though anxious not to take an active role in the company for fear of being accused of favouritism by other towns on the line where similar corn markets were held, nevertheless leased it a suitable and prominent site, near to the station and, for a long period of years, at a very low rent. The directors then 'set to work, and a very commodious brick building, of large dimensions, was erected, and although it is at present in a very unfinished state, it was sufficiently advanced to be opened on Tuesday last'.

The official opening was on Tuesday 20 October 1857. Business on that day started at noon and trade was brisk, enough to guarantee success. The *Journal* stated 'that there were 200 persons in the Corn Exchange'. All the local farming names were there: Revd J. Clutterbuck of Long Wittenham; J. Prowse; the Louseleys; the Humphreys; Abbott, Dandridge, Lovegrove, Tame, etc. Business concluded for the day, the assembled company adjourned to the Railway Hotel, where a large tent had been set up in the grounds, and dinner was served by Mrs Giles, the hotelier.

The Chairman's opening speech makes it only too clear how the local producers appreciated the value of the railway in conveying their corn to market. Before the railway, this area was relatively isolated, and previous means of marketing their crops, such as the stagecoach, the broad wheeled wagon with its six horses, and the canal, were cumbersome, slow and expensive. The railway had completely transformed their lives as producers; they now had a quick, efficient and relatively inexpensive method of getting to market. The establishment of the Corn Exchange had created a market that was next to the railway, and equally close to a fertile area of production. Dealers could now get to Didcot quickly and easily by railway, whereas before, the previous means of travel, the stagecoach, would have been impractical. Dealer and producer could meet, buy and sell to everyone's satisfaction. Eventually, dealers were coming from Worcester, Birmingham, Monmouth and South Wales; and in later years wool buyers for the big wool markets were coming from as far away as Bradford and the West Riding. The Junction Hotel registers for 1889 show that these buyers were coming from Yorkshire; and that the hotel was maintaining sixteen post horses that were in constant use that year conveying dealers to the East Ilsley Sheep Fair. Often accommodation at the station hotels was insufficient, so extra rooms were found at Blagrave Farm.

The Corn Exchange was a runaway success. Its very success led to a new and fresh development of the station area: practically all the buildings (other than the Junction Hotel) that surrounded it date from the years immediately after the establishment of the exchange. Each market day was frantically busy, with a bustling throng packing the station area, where dealers, farmers, their employees and workers, and others would meet. It may be that some form of traditional market formed on market days, attracting and selling to customers from neighbouring villages. It seems logical to assume that something of that kind may have existed.

By 1862, all the buildings flanking the Corn Exchange had been erected: the Prince of Wales Hotel; The Royal Oak, a new public house; a shop, bakehouse, and a house, owned and run by James Pryor of Harwell; and in Old Didcot, a new and the village's first pub, the Queen's Arms.

Such was the commercial activity generated that by 1865 two important banks felt there was sufficient business to warrant opening branches; these were the London and County Banking Company (later amalgamated with the Westminster in 1919) and the Wallingford Old Bank (Hedges, Wells & Co.; incorporated into Lloyds in 1905).

The Royal Oak, built in the late 1850s, and another Taunt postcard of c. 1905.

The first shop at the station was built by John Edward Pryor in 1860. It was opened in response to the trade generated by the Corn Exchange.

(Basil Pryor)

The increase in vehicular traffic, coming from all directions, via the Wantage Road, Park Lane, New Road and the Wallingford Road, on market days, soon prompted the Turnpike Trustees to erect two new gates: the Park Lane Bar which stopped up that road (it was sited near the modern roundabout), and the Hagbourne Gate (sited outside the entry to what is now Rich's Sidings). The Hagbourne Gate also had a tollhouse. The turnpikes had been installed by 1861.

In July 1861, a young man came to Didcot to work as a ticket clerk at the station. His name was Ernest J. Simmons; and in later life he wrote of his experiences as a stationmaster in an anonymously published book titled *Memoirs of a Stationmaster*, by Ernest Struggles, of 1879.

Ernest Simmons wrote anonymously because such was his fear of libel actions that he disguised every place and personal name under pseudonyms: Didcot Junction becomes 'Puzzle Junction' and John Peach, the Stationmaster, is 'Mr. Mulberry'.

He arrived at Didcot Station; and the first thing he did was insult Mr Peach by addressing him as 'Mr. Gooseberry', as 'Old Gooseberry' was his nickname. He described this early Didcot stationmaster by saying, 'I could but not notice my future master's extraordinary gait and appearance. Although very tall, he lost quite two inches by stooping, and with his aquiline hard features and straight hair . . .'.

Now at Didcot, he described the station as he saw it in July 1861:

> but I will first describe the station itself. It was a junction, and passengers changed there, I might say, for everywhere on the Great Smash Railway. The trains from the west came there to meet trains from the north, and vice versa. Stopping trains shunted there for express trains to pass them; the cheap trains up and both shunted for an hour and half, as it was the practice in those days to run one cheap or third-class train only in each direction, and to make that train shunt and stop as often as possible, in order to make people pay second-class and express fares.
>
> No one who travelled third class in those days was apparently entitled to a particle of respect, and the third class carriages were little better than cattle trucks. What with the stopping, changing and starting, Puzzle Junction was a very busy place. The station itself was like a dirty old barn, with both ends knocked out to allow the trains to run through; the roofing was black with smoke, and the paint all

> blistered. There were four roads for trains to stand under this roofing, or, strictly speaking, in the station, and five very narrow platforms.
>
> The only communication between the platforms was by means of an underground passage, so that supposing you alighted on platform 1, and wanted to go to platform 4, you had to go down a little trapway passage entrance, pass under nos. 2 and 3, and come up again at no. 4.
>
> The passage itself was simply filthy, as the leakage from the engines, as they stood waiting, caused a continual trickling of water which corroded on the walls in a slimy coating, sufficient to spoil any clothes that came in contact with them. There were some directions painted on the walls below which no one appeared to understand, besides half the passengers did not know if they were going north, south, or west; thus the directions described the platforms, and as no one was below to direct the passengers, they invariably came up at the wrong entrance, and had to go back and up again until they came to the right platform, often missing their train. . . .
>
> The station itself was above the ordinary level of the road by some twenty steps, but the booking office was on the ground level, and communciated with the mouth of the underground passage before referred to. . . . The number of tickets was ten times as large as that at Wilderness Road (or Wallingford Road); the booking was of a different nature, as the people for the most part booked to Puzzle Junction and then re-booked to some other station, all coming together, and all wanting to be waited on first.
>
> The tickets very much puzzled me. Numerous as they were, they did not cover one-half of the stations on the Great Smash Railway, it being the custom to print tickets only to those stations for which there was a frequent issue. A book was provided with a blank form of ticket, and I had to fill up one of these tickets when a passenger wished to go to a station for which I had no tickets printed.

It was this ticket system that caused Simmons to describe Didcot as Puzzle Junction; to say that it was slow and cumbersome would be an understatement. Today, passengers buy a ticket to their ultimate destination, irrespective of how many train changes they may have to make. But in Simmons's day, a ticket was bought every time a train was changed, so that during his first week he had a continual line of irate passengers queuing for tickets while their trains were poised above waiting or about to leave. Another problem was that as

> he was the only visible official at the entrance of this sudden bend to the tunnel foot passage, no one ever omitted to enquire of me as to which was the way they had to go to the train for this and that station.

He, during that first week, knew no more than they did, so he ignored them.

When stationed at Wallingford Road, he had comfortable lodgings, but it was far more difficult to find suitable accommodation at Didcot. He had been staying at the Junction Hotel, but at £60 p.a., it was far too expensive, when considering his annual salary of £70 a year. So he had to start looking for lodgings again. He asked around, but was told

> it was simply impossible to find any, for Puzzle was only a small village, and the engine drivers, porters, guards had already monopolised every house in the place. My search for a sleeping room was in vain, and I was about to give up when, as a last resource, I thought I would enquire at a little pub called 'The Owl and Moon'.

He was given a room which, unfortunately, lay over the tap room; although he did hear complimentary remarks from the porters. This pub was probably the old White Hart that formerly stood at the top of Station Road.

He did relate one interesting story concerning the rivalry between the two station hotels:

> it was quite a gala day at Puzzle Junction, for the new room for refreshments was to be opened that day. There had been a smart encounter between the newly built hotel and the old hotel, but Mrs Jones (Giles) of the old hotel, who had kept Mr Mulberry supplied with jelly and soup during his illness, had beaten Mr McGregor (Peter Playfair) of the new hotel, who was a penurious scotchman, and who was never known to give anything away but a pinch of snuff. So Mrs Jones, who had two marriageable daughters was duly installed as lessee of the refreshment room at £200 per annum, whereas the two McGregor girls were doomed to disappointment. The two families never spoke of one another from that date, except in disrespect, which was everlastingly sealed by old McGregor dying and leaving widow and daughters versus widow and daughters.

Having observed the antics of the widows and their daughters, a tale that would have been untold had it not been for the observations of Ernest Simmons, he left Didcot or Puzzle Junction to continue his career as a stationmaster at Aynho, in May 1863.

2

The Village of Didcot, 1839–1880

In 1839, the village community was subjected to what can only be described as a period of great traumatic change, for not only was that large gang of navvies laying the railway down through Didcot, with all the attendant disruption, but the landlords at the same time were pushing through the enclosure of Didcot's open fields. The abandonment of open field farming at a time when the village as a whole was still recovering from the upheavals caused by the navvies, must have laid great stress upon the village community, where traditional farming methods in those fields had been handed down from father to son, from generation to generation. The open fields had been a part of the scenery of Didcot for over a thousand years; suddenly, at the behest of a few landlords, the villagers were told to give up their traditional ways – cooperative ploughing, the annual rotation, headlands, furlongs, yardlands, the long doles, all the paraphernalia of the open fields – to cope with new ideas and new methods, all in the name of efficiency and profit. They also had to give up their common right to gather fuel in The Hadden, the village wood (this used to cover the ridge on the opposite side of Cow Lane, on the other side of the Abingdon Road), a right which was translated into the yearly coal charity issued at Christmas. There must have been quite a period of adjustment before the new systems became the norm. Another event of 1840 was the commutation of the tithes into a yearly payment, though this did not affect the villagers. However, the enclosure and the tithe commutation gave us two invaluable records: the Enclosure and Tithe Awards, and their maps. The two documents, with the Census for 1841, give us a complete record of the village in the 1840s.

Another event of the 1840s, though one no doubt welcomed by the male community as a whole, was the final abandonment of the View of Frankpledge or the Tithing, which was another anachronism of the Middle Ages. No longer would all males between the ages of 12 and 70 have to attend the Frankpledge Court, usually held at Ardington. As most men did not, they were compelled to 'essoign' or default, and pay the tithing penny, which was deeply resented. The Tithing went in 1847. The final event of the 1840s, already described, was the opening of Didcot Junction in 1844.

Truly it could be said that the events of those two decades, events that occurred almost one after another, make that period one of the most important in Didcot's long history.

The major landowners in 1839 were the Revd R.P. Morrell, John Blagrave, Revd W.R. Baker, Richard Cummins, Robert Hopkins, the Revd Joseph Hodgkinson (the Rector), William Taylor, the Revd J.H. Best, and Queen's College, Oxford.

Morrells Farm, of 232 acres, centred on its farmhouse, with barns and other outbuildings, was formerly located in Foxhall Road, opposite the modern Brasenose Road. This farm complex, other than the largest barn, now the home of the Conservative Club, was demolished after the Second World War. The Morrell tenants during the period up to 1880 were John Smith, 1826–50, then Fred Dandridge to his death in 1856. After he died, his widow, Julia, took over the tenancy. She remarried and her new husband, James Greenaway, became the next tenant; this was before 1868. During the late 1870s, the tenancy then passed to George Napper, a member of that prolific late nineteenth-century family, the Nappers of East and West Hagbourne.

The Blagrave family, who were very probably connected to the Blagraves of Reading, had owned the farm at Didcot since 1784. After the enclosure, in which they must have been prime movers, the farm's acreage increased to 203 acres. Their farmhouse, in Lydalls Road, is still known to this day as 'Blagrave's Farm'. Although the house still exists, the barns and other outbuildings were demolished after the last war. The Blagrave tenants during the same period up to 1880, were John Hayward, 1835–42, Robert Summers, 1842–9, and Benjamin Leach 1849–57. After Leach gave up the tenancy, it passed to Thomas Buckle in 1858, but he only rented a part of the farm, which seems to have been split into three sections, each one held by a

Foxhall Road, 1905, with the buildings of Manor Farm on the left.

different tenant. The farmhouse was occupied by the Buckles. At the end of the 1860s, Mrs Jane Giles, formerly of the Junction Hotel, had taken over the main part of the Blagrave tenancy. She gave up the lease to the Junction Hotel in 1870, which was then held by George Drewe. Also it seems that by that year she had left Didcot, though still a Blagrave tenant. By 1880, the tenancy once more had changed hands; this time the tenant was a James Turner.

The third landowner in order of acreage held was the Revd William R. Baker, Lord and owner of the Manor of Didcot, and of Manor Farm, whose farm size in 1840 was 178 acres. The farmhouse, now sheltered accommodation for old people, still stands in Foxhall Road. William Baker inherited the manor and farm from his brother. His great-uncle John had purchased the property from Henry Blake earlier in 1778. William Baker was another of those landlords who had pushed through the enclosure in 1840. His tenant in that year was James Dunsden, one of the Dunsden family, who had held this important tenancy since the 1780s, and as such were leaders of that village community during the early to mid-nineteenth century. This almost premier position came through the long continuity of years during which the tenancy had been held. They were only eclipsed by the Taylors, in particular, William Taylor of Taylors Farm. James Dunsden was the tenant in 1840, having succeeded to the lease two years earlier, after the death of his father, William. Previously, James had held the lease to Ladygrove Farm (off the Abingdon Road), which he gave up in favour of Henry, his younger brother. The family held a number of other tenancies. Another brother, William, was the licencee of Didcot's first public house, and the first of the two White Harts; this was at New House. It too was owned by the Revd Baker. James Dunsden's two sisters also owned the house (now 29–31 Manor Road), which at that time was occupied by one of the Woodleys, another prolific local family (of which a great many are still living in Didcot and the surrounding villages); he was George Woodley, who at that time was the village blacksmith. James died in 1848 aged 60; as he never married, the tenancy was taken over by another brother, William, the former publican at the White Hart. William died twenty years later in 1868, having outlived all his brothers. And with his death, the Dunsden connection with Didcot finally ended. The lease then passed to Henry Buckle, who at the same time was renting Foxhall. The next tenant was Benjamin Leach; he was still holding the lease in 1880. Not only did tenancies change, so did land ownership. The Revd Baker sold the lordship and the manor of Didcot, with Manor Farm, to Lord Overstone in 1857. Manor Farm then consisted of Manor Farmhouse, New House, two cottages (now 23 Manor Road), two barns, the blacksmith's shop, and 186 acres of land.

Richard Cummins had died by 1840 and his property, Foxhall Farm, of 91 acres, was held by his trustees. William Hale had been his tenant from 1840, having succeeded Edward Pullen; he was the one assaulted by the navvies in the previous year. Hale held the tenancy until 1849, which passed to John Guy, and then to John Hull. In 1857–8, Foxhall was purchased by Jacob Appleford, who became an owner-occupier. He was both farmer and a collector of antiques, which he used to adorn and improve his house. Many years before the house, or that very 'fine Tudor residence', was finally demolished in 1883, Appleford had bought and installed oak panelling for the hall and stairs.

In 1868, Foxhall Farm was sold to Colonel Loyd-Lindsay, Lord Overstone's son-in-law. As noted above, Henry Buckle had been tenant in the early 1870s. But by 1880, the larger part of the farmland was attached to that of Manor Farm, when rented by Benjamin Leach.

In 1839, Robert Hopkins owned Ladygrove Farm, at that time a farm of 84 acres. The farmhouse still exists; it is probably the most attractive period house in Didcot and dates back to the sixteenth century. It is probably never seen by anyone other than its owners, as it is approached by a long private lane. The tenant in 1839 was Henry Dunsden. The lease had previously been held by his brother, James, who gave it up on the death of their father, William. Henry remained tenant to 1845, dying two years later. He was followed at Ladygrove by a succession of tenants, who only held the lease for short periods, such as Charles and George Lyford, to 1853, James Leaver to 1858, and William Hayward to 1864. The latter may well have been that William Hayward of Long Wittenham, who was both Chairman of the Didcot Corn Exchange, and a prime mover in its establishment in 1857.

Robert Hopkins's trustees presumably sold the farm during the 1840s. In 1864, the owner was James Prowse, who was a corn dealer. The farm was sold by him to St John's College, Oxford, and they in turn sold it to Lord Overstone, in 1867. After which Ladygrove never had a separate identity as a farm ever again. The farmhouse was rented out, usually to farm workers, and the land attached to other, larger Didcot farms.

Another small farm in 1839 was Bests Farm in Manor Road (now 28–30 Manor Road), and owned in 1839 by the Revd James Best. The Best family had acquired the Didcot farm through marriage, to a daughter of the Revd Head Pottinger. He bought the farm in 1787. Later, in 1840, its extent was 32 acres; and in that year, its tenant William Webb. He had held the lease since 1832. After his death, his widow, Jane, took over the tenancy, which she held until she lost the lease in 1851. The next tenant was Thomas Buckle, who was also holding a part of Foxhall Farm. He, and after his death in 1861, Sophia, his widow, continued with the tenancy (she too was still holding part of Foxhall), until their son, Henry, came of age in 1870. He did not hold the lease very long, as it soon passed to another of the Napper clan, William Napper, in 1874. Bests Farm was another of those Didcot farms that was purchased by Lord Overstone in 1869.

The other remaining farms at Didcot in 1839 were those of William Taylor, Queen's College and the Rector's Glebe. They can be bracketed together because throughout this period they were leased together as one farm.

William had inherited the Taylor farm from his formidable father in 1826. The Taylors were undoubtedly pre-eminent in Didcot. Not only were they still living in the parish as owners of a large farm, they were not absentee landlords, as were all the others. They had been a dominant force in village life since the late eighteenth century. William Taylor not only held his own farm of 85 acres, he was also holding the leases to the Queen's College farm, 67 acres, and the Rector's Glebe, which was another 78 acres; and with three smallholdings, the total acreage was 234 acres, which made the Taylor farm the largest in Didcot. It was even bigger than John Blagrave's farm.

William Taylor died in 1866 and during the next year his trustees sold the Taylor farm to the Revd Thomas Rennison of Queen's College (he was the college bursar) and Henry Smith became his tenant; hence the modern name of 'Smiths Farm' – even though the Smiths left Didcot in the 1920s. The death of William Taylor brought to an end the long association of this family with Didcot, almost an era, a period of at least 340 years. Henry Smith, like William Taylor, his predecessor, continued to hold the tenancies of Queen's College and the glebe; however, he was soon to lose the latter.

The other farms, if they can be called that, were really smallholdings, such as those owned by Thame School, Edward Johnson, the

Revd J.D. Murray, and Edward Smith. The largest of these was not more than 8 acres; and all were rented and added to larger farms. Edward Johnson and Edward Smith owned cottages rather than land.

In the early 1850s, Lord Overstone arrived in North Berkshire, after the Manor of East Lockinge had been purchased by his father, Lewis Loyd, in 1854; although they were both still living at the family seat of Overstone Park, near Northampton.

Lord Overstone is important in the history of Didcot and that of surrounding villages, such as Blewbury and the Hagbournes, as it was he who began the process of building the vast Loyd estate in North Berkshire during the late nineteenth century. After 1859, its owner was that outstanding man, Colonel Loyd-Lindsay, later Lord Wantage of West Lockinge, and Lord Overstone's son-in-law. The impact of these two men on North Berkshire cannot be overstated.

Samuel Jones Loyd, Lord Overstone, was the son of Lewis Loyd, an eminent banker of the early nineteenth century. His was a famous bank in the City during this period, Jones, Loyd & Company. When he died in 1858, he left an estate valued at £3 million.

His son, Samuel Jones Loyd, entered the family firm as a partner in 1818, after the finish of his education. He soon gained a reputation as one of the shrewder and outstandingly intelligent of the new generation of young bankers. His influence, both on the development of the theory of banking and on government policy, became considerable after 1832. He was Member of Parliament for Hythe from 1819 to 1826; although he seemed destined for politics, his temperament was such, a nervousness that almost bordered on timidity, that made him totally unsuited for the tumult of politics. But he was viewed with great awe during his lifetime for the decisive way that he dealt with all arguments and problems. To the world he assumed an aloof and unapproachable manner, which only covered a sensitive nature.

He, like many other businessmen of the period, soon found city life irksome and wished to retire to the country, even when he was at the height of his career as a highly influential banker. He started this move in the 1830s, by purchasing land in Buckinghamshire. In 1850, he was offered a barony, and became Lord Overstone; he then handed over his banking interests to his younger cousins. He was now free to develop the Lockinge Estate, purchased previously by his father, Lewis Loyd, in 1854.

After the marriage of his daughter, Harriet, to Lieutenant-Colonel

Robert Loyd-Lindsay (he adopted his bride's surname, hence the addition of Loyd) in 1859, Lord Overstone settled on the young couple the Manor of East Lockinge as a marriage gift. Other properties were added to the seat, such as the Manor of Didcot, and Manor Farm, acquired by Lord Overstone earlier, in 1857. He had also purchased the Manor of East Hagbourne in the same year. Other Didcot farms were also added to the estate in the 1860s, purchased by either Lord Overstone or Col. Loyd-Lindsay: Ladygrove Farm, 1867; Foxhall Farm, 1868; and Bests Farm, 1869. By 1873, Col. Loyd-Lindsay owned 368 acres, which made him the owner with the largest acreage in Didcot.

Every human community is made up of buildings and people: at Didcot village in 1839, the buildings in the main were primitive, and the people poor. Practically all the houses at the time of enclosure were obviously timber-framed, and it is significant that having existed for hundreds of years without change, many were demolished within the next two decades: was this for economic reasons, creating space so that brick cottages could be built in their place? (Certainly, the newcomers, the railwaymen, did have money for renting, but not for the hovels that existed in 1839.) Or were they demolished in response to the liberal social ideas that were influencing the middle classes during these two decades? By 1880, nine houses/cottages had gone, either demolished or burnt down. Fire had destroyed three properties within the space of seven years, including the Queen's College farmhouse in Manor Road in 1844. Another cottage was destroyed in 1839, by a deaf and dumb boy playing with matches, and the other, in Lydalls Road, was noted in the Tithe Award as burnt down. There were two cottages in the Waste (this was the early name used for that part of Manor Road, opposite Manor Cottage); they had been removed by 1857. Other cottages, two in Manor Road, and one in Lydalls Road, had also been demolished by 1880. Fortunately, a photograph exists for the last one to go; it shows it to have been a cruck, timber-framed house of the late fourteenth or early fifteenth century; and it was one of the two 'messuages' left to Queen's College in 1498. This was the last Didcot timber-framed house – as indeed were all those mentioned above – to have been demolished up until the modern day.

Another complex to be demolished was the sixteenth-century rectory house and barns, especially the Tithe Barn, which had been in a ruinous state since the early eighteenth century and no longer needed after commutation of tithes in 1841. The rectory house, which is

White Cottage in Manor Road; a cruck cottage of the fifteenth century, which survived, purely by chance, the demolitions of the 1840s. *(C.T. Milne)*

The 'new' Rectory of 1851, as designed by H.J. Underwood, and built by the Rector, Revd John Ashwood. It replaced an earlier sixteenth-century-building. (Don Farnborough)

assumed to have been sixteenth century in date, was built in an 'E' shape, according to the Enclosure Award, and was sited a little to the south-east of the second rectory house. The Tithe Barn fronted Lydalls Road on the north side; its site is now that of modern bungalows. These buildings were removed after the arrival of the new Rector, the Revd John A. Ashworth, who was a resident. It was he who demolished the old rectory house, which had been described in the 1730s as ruinous, and replaced it with a new Rectory. The Rector employed Mr H.J. Underwood as architect; he was a pupil of Sir Robert Smirke, architect of the British Museum. This Victorian building is no longer the Rectory and has been converted in recent years into flats. Ashworth also demolished the Tithe Barn and other outbuildings, and landscaped the grounds with lawns and flowerbeds.

The junction was opened in 1844, and immediately afterwards there was an influx of railwaymen and their families into Didcot. No effort was made to provide housing, certainly not within the rest of that decade. The first housing to be provided were the cottages erected at the top of Station Road, or 'The Hill', by, it seems, the GWR, although a James Ploughman, in those early years, was always given as the owner. They were called The Ploughman Buildings in 1861. In later years, their name was Mount Pleasant, but known colloquially as 'The Barracks'. In those early years, up to the 1870s, the large white house that fronted the cottages was built as the stationmaster's house. This is where Mr Peach, the stationmaster, who was described by Ernest Simmons as 'Mr Mulberry', lived in 1861.

The next development was in the village, where, in 1858, seemingly as a reaction to the opening of the Corn Exchange, a large number of working-class cottages was erected. But, almost certainly, they were built as a response to the large influx of railway workers into Didcot during the 1850s. In July 1857, an expanded brick-built engine shed was opened that replaced the earlier wooden shed of 1844; presumably this brought many new workers to Didcot. The Censuses of 1851 and 1861 show a dramatic increase in their number during that decade. In 1851, there were 15 railway workers living in Didcot; ten years later this number had risen to 51, after which there was no appreciable rise in the workforce, certainly not by 1871, when there were just 54; and two of these were telegraph clerks. The number of dependants also rose: in 1851, there were 32, but by 1861 this figure had jumped to 87. But ten years later, this number had dropped to 76, with a corresponding fall in family numbers. As a percentage of the population, the railwaymen and families were, in 1851, 19.5 per cent (241); in 1861, 39.54 per cent (349); and in 1871, 35.23 per cent (369). With this increase, landlords were soon building cottages for the railwaymen: cottages which would quickly bring in a rent revenue. The earlier structures were, of course, rent free to the farm workers, and as such hardly worth replacing, and were certainly not acceptable to the newcomers.

Many of the early Victorian cottages in the village, built with railwaymen in mind, date to the years 1858–9. Two semi-detached pairs were erected in the 1860s. The majority of these have now been demolished. Most were sited in Manor Road: nos 43 to 49 were erected by the Revd R.P. Morrell in 1858, and on his own land. The timber-framed house formerly standing there was demolished. These were built in stone. But the pair immediately next door to the east, nos 39 to 41, are not only different in style – built in brick – but also in date. These were built by the Revd Thomas Rennison, owner of Smiths Farm, but on Queen's College land, and date to 1869–70. The Revd Morrell also built another pair of cottages, in 1858, architecturally of the same date as nos 43 to 49; these stood formerly in

Smiths Lane (now Brasenose Road), opposite the farmyard of Smiths Farm. Farther down the road, opposite White Cottage, was another semi-detached pair, built by John Blagrave, in *c.* 1862. Below White Cottage, on the north side of Manor Road, was a terrace of seven cottages, erected in 1858–9 by the Revd Charles Hemmings. These were replaced by a modern terrace built by the Blakes in the early 1960s. Next to the Hemmings terrace, separated by the track which exits there from Lydalls Road, was another set of three cottages that were attached to the Queen's Arms and are of the same date. Around the corner, in Lydalls Road and almost opposite Blagrave's Farm, stands another terrace of four cottages, nos 117 to 123 Lydalls Road, built in 1858, by a James Banwell, a railway carriage fitter. He must have come to Didcot from Somerset as a young man when the station opened, and stayed in the village until he died in 1908. He was also the owner of a terrace of four cottages, this time in Northbourne, sited in the Broadway, nos 115 to 121, erected 1874.

Another house in Northbourne, 5 Mereland Road, was also erected by James in 1870. He was obviously well off, with several properties out to rent, but, strangely, he chose to live in lodgings in Didcot village, when he was rich enough to live very comfortably, and marry. Servants were easy to come by; in 1851, the Census reveals, for instance, that a William Brassington, a railway guard, employed a young female servant. Although many in the village, other than labourers, had servants.

The Queen's Arms, was another building that was erected directly in response to the surge in the village population during the late 1850s; its building date is 1858–9. The first owner was a John Carter; and his tenant, and the first publican, Joseph Stanmore. He was succeeded by Henry Sired to 1883, by Mrs Hannah Shippen, 1895, by George Lewis, 1900, and by his widow, Mrs Harriet Lewis. The pub's ownership also changed, and by *c.* 1870, was acquired by Field & Co., presumably a brewery firm.

Another house to be built during this early period was Britwell Lodge. It is easy enough to find out who was its builder, John Blagrave; that it was built on his land; and that its first tenant was a William Wignell; even further that it was built in 1850. But thc question that is impossible to answer is why was it built? Was it designed to be a country villa for a gentleman? Commuting must have started early on, for the railway then and now did mean that men could live some way away from their work. The house never functioned as a

Another set of Victorian cottages, this time in Manor Road, nos 39–41 and 43–9, built respectively by Revd Thomas Rennison in 1869–70, and Revd R.P. Morrell in 1858.

Lydalls Road. The cottages, nos 117–23, seen in the middle of the illustration, were those erected by James Banwell in 1858.

The Queen's Arms pictured here about the time of the First World War. It was another of those buildings to be erected in the late 1850s.

farmhouse, although it did have land attached, and was always a gentleman's residence. William Wignell was followed in the tenancy by his widow Emma. By 1865, the house had been purchased by Mrs Mary Newton; it was she who named it Blenheim House. She lived in the house until the late 1870s, after which it was let to Thomas Freeguard and Carl Alson. Then in *c.* 1889, it was sold to Arthur Stevens; he renamed the house Britwell Lodge, its present-day name. Interestingly, in the 1871 Census, it was called Britwell Lodge, although the earlier name continued to be used into the 1880s.

That the arrival of the railwaymen during the 1840s and 1850s had a cultural impact on the village and its people is without doubt. The villagers were still living in a semi-feudal state, subject to the will of squire and parson, and certainly not economically free. They lived in tied houses; any signs of dissension could mean dismissal, and the horror of parish relief or even the workhouse. By contrast, the railwaymen, though they might live in the village, either next door or even as lodgers, to the villagers, were economically free. The gap, economic and social, between a tenant farmer and one of his labourers

Britwell Lodge in Britwell Road. A Victorian villa of 1852.

was huge and unbridgeable. A tenant farmer could be enjoying an income ten times as great as that of one of his labourers. The Rector was receiving an income of about £500 a year. Presumably, the farmers enjoyed similar incomes. The census papers reveal just how prosperous they were: they were all employing servants. Julia Dandridge had living in a governess, a nurse, one female and three male farm labourers, a shepherd, etc. Each farmer enjoyed the comforts of a large house, while his labourers and their families were living two or even three to a cottage: the Nook in Church Path, now the home of one family, in 1861 was housing three, at a total of sixteen people.

The gap between the stationmaster and his employees was not so great, economically at least. Mr Peach, the stationmaster in 1861, was not greatly respected – at least, if Ernest Simmons in his *Memoirs of a Stationmaster* is to be believed. He was receiving, as a probationary clerk, £60 p.a.; when established he would receive another £10. Simmons also says that the salary for a junior stationmaster was £80 p.a. The pay of a junior engine-drive, or night cleaner, was 10*s*. to 14*s*. per week.

Church Lane and the Nook in about 1907. The cottage at that time was occupied by three families; now it is the home of just one family. (*Don Farnborough*)

There can be no doubt that in relation to the village working class railway men were far more prosperous. This can be seen, indirectly, by the number of tradesmen who set up shop in Didcot during the period. In 1841, there was a shopkeeper, a blacksmith and a publican. Twenty years later, there were two grocers, a master butcher, a baker, a dressmaker, four publicans, and the blacksmith. It is no coincidence that the village school started up in 1847, and continued without a break until the board school was established in 1894; the railwaymen, presumably, could afford the fees, and gave their children the opportunity to be educated. Although everyone who had room was not above taking in lodgers. The majority of the railway employees were young men, mostly under 25, single, and lodging in the village. They were crammed into almost every cottage. When Ernest Simmons arrived, he found it very difficult to find lodgings. Eventually he ended up in the pub.

Though by 1861 the railwaymen made up well over a third of the village population, they did not form a majority. Didcot was still an agricultural community, with farming the main economic activity. Most of the men worked as agricultural labourers: farms at that time were labour intensive. Julia Dandridge at Morrells Farm (250 acres) employed 8 men and 3 boys, and William Dunsden at Manor Farm (170 acres), 9 men and 2 boys. There were 37 agricultural labourers living in Didcot in 1861.

To service their needs in 1861, there were two shops, a butcher and a baker. The village shop had always been in Manor Road and had functioned as such since the early eighteenth century. In 1841, the shopkeeper was a John Bosher, who rented the premises from William Taylor. Bosher gave way about 1849 to John Andrews, who as Didcot's shopkeeper, also maintained the post office. He had died by 1873, the shop now under the control of Elizabeth, his widow; the owner was now Mrs Giles. Later, Miss Ann Appleford, daughter of Jacob, took over.

The other shop in 1861 was maintained by a Mrs Webb, and was a front-parlour shop. There were many of these in the nineteenth century: there were several in Northbourne, but only two in the village. The butcher in 1861 was James Appleford, who had his shop in New House; he was the brother of Jacob Appleford at Foxhall. The baker in the same year was a William Butcher, who was operating another front-parlour shop – but he did not last long. The village had therefore undergone great changes during those twenty years following the opening of Didcot Junction. Many of the early timber-framed cottages had been demolished, but the streets remained and are the same as those of today.

Manor Road was then known as the 'Waste', later as 'High Street' and round by the 'Queens' it was Queens Street. Lydalls Road was then Lydalls Lane.

We can leave Amy Strange, who died in August 1950 and remembered her youth vividly, to sum up Didcot as she knew it at that time. This extract comes from an article written for the *Didcot Advertizer* in 1950 by S. Allen Warner:

> as a girl, Amy regularly attended the church in the old village. She recalled the times when after rain the lanes were so deep in mud that they became well-nigh impassable unless one wore pattens. Remembering the length of dresses in those days, and knowing that pattens only raised you a very few inches above the ground, one can picture what a washing and brushing there would be on a Monday in those days of long ago.
>
> Amy Strange never tired of telling of these olden times. She not only remembered Didcot called Dudcot [as it was known then], but with a twinkle in her eye used to say that Mudcot would have been as good as any – in the winter time!

3

North Hagbourne alias Didcot New Town, 1868–1900

The origins of Didcot New Town, or North Hagbourne, or Northbourne as it is generally known today, began in 1839, with the enclosure of East Hagbourne's open field system. An allotment of 89 acres in East Hagbourne's Upper and Lower End Fields was granted to Thomas Higgs. After he died in 1855, his will was challenged by relatives in the Court of Chancery, and eventually that court ordered that Higgs's estate be sold by public auction; this took place at the Junction Hotel, at Didcot Station, when the estate was sold in two lots, on 24 July 1865. Lot 1, of 120 acres, including the 89 acre allotment, was sold to Stephen Dixon, a farmer, of Parsonage Farm, East Hagbourne. He paid £6,130. It was agreed that the balance of the purchase price should be paid by November 1866; to do this he had to arrange a mortgage, which he negotiated with Edward Ormond, a solicitor, and others, all of Wantage, for £3,825. This mortgage was to become an enormous burden for Dixon, one which he never discharged, and was still unpaid at the time of his death.

However, Dixon was not the first to start building in Northbourne. Earlier, in 1863, a small allotment of land adjoining the railway line, immediately adjacent to the Marsh Bridge arch, was sold in December that year to George Napper, a builder, of East Hagbourne. (He was Dennis Napper's father. He eventually inherited these cottages.) It was on this piece of land that Napper built two sets of cottages, the Marsh and Railway Terraces, in 1864. One terrace, known as Marsh Cottages, is sited along the line of a track that runs up beside the railway and faces it. The other set of cottages,

Marsh Cottages (or Railway Terrace as they were originally known), erected by George Napper in 1863, and photographed in the early 1960s.
(Miss C. Purdy)

known then as 'Railway Terrace', face the main road. They have now lost their former name.

Besides these cottages is a child's playground, with swings, etc. It was most likely donated by George Napper to the East Hagbourne Church of St Andrews, and was probably land left over after his building operations had ended. It was a very generous gesture really, especially when the only children who could possibly use it at that time were those living in the cottages immediately adjacent. It is even more odd, considering the amount of open places and the road in which they could play. The recreation ground is still enjoyed by children; and is administered today by the Didcot Town Council.

Within the next year, 1867, Dixon started selling building plots – there were twelve – some of which fronted the south side of Wallingford Road, with the others at the top of Hagbourne Road, opposite Rich's Sidings.

It is not entirely clear if Dixon initiated these early land sales himself or whether he was approached by potential buyers, and thus given the idea by those who wished to build in their various ways. Possibly, the existence of that enormous mortgage compelled him to sell. He was, after all, a farmer and not a builder. But there was a demand from those who wanted to build, from those who wished to rent out houses and from those who wanted to rent. Obviously, Dixon must have been aware of the profits that could be made from selling the land in these small lots and, eventually, from building and renting houses; also, he must have been equally aware of the housing famine that existed then, and of the potential demand for houses to rent. So he was soon not only selling land, but building and renting in his own right; and thus the next stage in the development of Didcot had begun.

It was not long before he, too, was holding land auctions at the Junction Hotel; and it was then that these twelve lots were sold. The first of these sales was in 1867, another in October 1868.

The earliest buildings in Northbourne, excluding the cottages at the railway arch, were the Primitive Methodist Chapel (now

The row of cottages in lower Church Street. Known at the end of the nineteenth century as 'Dixon's Row', and built by Stephen Dixon in 1870–3.

demolished; the site is occupied by Lays Electrical Shop), and the house immediately next door, to the east, 105–7 Broadway. This house has on its gable peak, 'W.H. 1867'; these letters are worn – the 'H' is really a 'W' – and are the initials of the builder, Warner West. He also built a further two houses (semi-detached pairs), that stood immediately to the west, now demolished. Another house to be erected in the same year was Newtown Cottage, by Henry Wright, a railway policeman, who became an owner-occupier. This house has also been demolished.

It was not long before he was laying down the course of Church Street, and the upper parts of Mereland Road and High Street; and this was as early as 1868. (For the building dates of houses in Northbourne see Appendix). Most of the houses in these roads predate 1875. By 1875, twenty sets of houses had been built, which ran in numbers from single detached houses to a terrace of twelve cottages. A small early Anglican church had also been built which, together with the primitive Methodist Chapel, shows how religious these railwaymen were.

As we have seen, Dixon was soon building in his own right. He started with the cottages in lower Church Street, which were then known as 'Dixons Row'. Eventually, he owned more than twenty cottages, including several shops, owning more than any other landlord.

Given this initial spurt, house building rapidly took off: in 1875, these twenty sets of housing actually comprised detached and semi-detached houses and terraces of three, four, eight and twelve cottages (in all there were fifty-nine housing units), and their number steadily increased during the remainder of the 1870s and into the 1880s. This was rapid progress considering the haphazard way in which they were built: one here, one there; there was no overall plan; the lots, presumably, were marked out and sold, and houses built when a prospective landlord or owner-occupier appeared.

Though some houses were built on behalf of owner-occupiers, most were for renting. Many houses and cottages were built speculatively by small jobbing builders – there were three or even four working at that time, such as Ephraim Child, Henry Turvey and G.H. Pilsham – who sold to clients, usually tradesmen, who used the rents as supplementary incomes. The names of most of these landlords, their occupations, and the number of houses they owned, were noted in the Sanitary Authority's minutes, in 1880.

Northbourne Landlords (Sanitary Authority's minutes, 1880)

Owner	Houses	Residence	Occupation
Dixon, Stephen	20	East Hagbourne	Farmer
Lay, John	8	Harwell	Farmer
Wood, Revd James	6	Wallingford	Builder
West, Warner	6	East Hendred	Dealer
Shepperd, E.L.	4	Abingdon	Ironmonger
Drewe, James	4	Didcot	Hotel keeper
Burnidge, John	3	Dorchester	Publican
Whiting, Edward	3	Sutton Courtenay	Dealer
Andrews, Thomas	3	East Hagbourne	Railway employee
Pilcher, James	1	East Hagbourne	Parish clerk
Wright, Henry	1	North Hagbourne	Railway employee
Pugh, George	1	North Hagbourne	Railway employee
Haynes, Robert	1	North Hagbourne	Railway employee
Marten, Jabez	1	North Hagbourne	Railway employee
Bosley, Mark	1	North Hagbourne	Railway employee
Sidery, Sarah	1	Lisbony, Torquay	Spinster

These sixteen landlords between them owned sixty-five houses. Quite obviously, the building work going on at Didcot must have been common knowledge throughout North Berkshire, to have attracted owner-landlords from these other localities.

Dixon did have a finger in every pie at Northbourne: he was also engaged in supplying bricks. An area north of the railway was formerly known as the 'Brickfields'; here in partnership with

W.H. Manning & Co., he set up kilns to make bricks, which were handmade and sun-dried by the old-fashioned method. This was set up right at the start of the building of Northbourne, as early as 1868. This does, show, to a certain extent, the way he was thinking, and his intentions at such an early stage in its history. He also built a row of four cottages, which became known as 'Brickfield Cottages', for the workers, in 1870. Unfortunately, it was found out later that these bricks were porous, and would not keep out rain. The clay from north of the railway was completely unsuitable for brick making. A detached pair of cottages, nos 21–3 Broadway, were built using these bricks, and water would soak through the walls during heavy rain-storms. Eventually, they were rendered with pebbledash to make them waterproof. The cottages were built *c.* 1895, and demolished *c.* 1990.

Dixon had laid out the course of all roads by the mid-1880s. Church Street and upper Mereland Road, or West Street as it was known then, had been in position since 1868, and by 1874 were recognizable roads. The western half of Wessex Road was laid down

Church Street at the beginning of the century. The cottages shown were erected between 1869 and 1903. *(Don Farnborough)*

later, in 1894–5. Hagbourne Road is different: in the 1860s and '70s, it was known as the 'Street'; it is an ancient road or track and dates back to the early medieval period, originally an access way from East Hagbourne village to its open fields, Lower End and Upper End Fields, which lay on both sides of the road. It also gave access to Hagbourne Marsh – East Hagbourne's common lands.

These roads were not given their present names until 1897. Before then, Wallingford Road was known both by that name and as the 'Upper Road', and Wessex Road as the 'Lower Road'. Houses and terrace blocks had their own individual names, such as Oxford Terrace (2–16) High Street; Newtown Terrace (29–41), in Broadway; and, of course, Marsh and Railway Terrace, near the railway arch. All houses were named: Highfield House (its site now Barclays Bank), Monkton House, Bonaventure and The Trinity in Mereland Road; Hope Cottage and Newtown Cottage in Broadway; Carey Cottage and East View in Hagbourne Road; and South View in Wessex Road.

In 1897, the East Hagbourne Parish Council was asked to name these streets officially – the Wallingford Rural District Council was applying to the Ministry of Health to make Northbourne part of a

Bourne Street. The houses shown were built in the 1880s.

Special Drainage Area and needed the roads named. The parish council did it very quickly, seemingly, in an evening, and came up with the most banal of names: West Street (Mereland Road); Church Street (previously High Street); High Street; East Street; South Street (now Wessex Road). Wallingford Road was unaltered. The cul-de-sac was named Block Street, and renamed Bourne Street in 1929.

Building plots were laid out early on and sold at differing times – at times by auction; equally, houses could differ in their year of construction even when sited next door to each other. This is why Northbourne was constructed in such an haphazard way. Obviously, the streets took on that appearance only after houses were constructed – with their terraces, blocks, semis and detached houses. It may be hard to believe, but these streets before 1898 were even narrower than they are today. In that year, the Rural District Council negotiated with house owners to widen the streets, by giving up part of the frontages. Many did so voluntarily – James Banwell dedicated 4 ft of a frontage in Church Street, next to 5 Mereland Road, while an equal number demanded payment. The Rural District Council wanted the streets to be at least 20 ft wide; and the width they finally did achieve can be seen today. In winter, before proper surfaces were laid down, roads were usually impassable due to thick mud that was constantly being churned up, and which was often mixed with escaping sewage.

Northbourne was built virtually during two decades, the 1870s and '80s; building had started as early as 1868, but the majority of houses were built in this period: Wallingford Road or Broadway, late 1860s, '70s and '80s; Church Street, mainly 1870s; High Street, 1870s and '80s; East Street, 1880s; Block or Bourne Street, 1880s; Hagbourne Road, early 1870s through into the next century. Houses were still being added in the 1890s and early 1900s, just the odd one in Hagbourne Road or South Street. Many of the plots had been sold early on and never built upon. The 1898 25 in. map shows many gaps. This is why Bourne Street is a cul-de-sac, which does not exit into West Street, because George Drewe had purchased the land previously and built the large house (9–13) in Mereland Road in 1880, thus preventing it. Therefore, Northbourne was virtually complete by 1887.

When a small estate such as that of Northbourne is built, its people need services such as churches, schools, shops and public houses, and these are soon provided.

The first of these to be supplied was the Primitive Methodist Chapel in the Wallingford Road, built in 1868. Other than the Marsh Cottages, it was the first building to be erected in Northbourne. The

Cottages in High Street, nos 4–16. This was another terrace erected by Stephen Dixon, from 1888 to 1883, and occupied by the élite of Northbourne, the engine-drivers.

trustees were well known in the area at that time, men such as Edward Wakefield, a grocer of East Hagbourne, Henry Wright, a railwayman, John Blissett, the Didcot blacksmith and George Hobbs, a coal merchant, also of Didcot. It was replaced as a chapel by the present Methodist church when that opened in 1903. Afterwards, the redundant chapel went through a number of uses: it was once a school, and a social club, before being demolished in the 1960s.

A temporary Anglican church had also existed, possibly erected *c.* 1870, before it too was replaced by the Church of St Peter's in 1891. It was originally built as a chapel of ease to St Andrew's Church in East Hagbourne, to serve the religious needs of Northbourne. The building of the church was mainly through the efforts of the Revd W.R. Baker, who aroused interest and collected money for the purpose. The project at one time looked as if it would fall through, and was finally carried out with the help of Robert Rich, who agreed to build the church at an extraordinarily low cost. He was both builder and architect. Lady Wantage gave the land.

The building of St Peter's Church in 1890.

The original contract for the building of the church was for £607. After the work was begun, it was decided to build the church longer by 5 ft than the length originally decided, and the total cost of the building was £869. There was no smithy nearby where tools could be sharpened so while building was in progress a boy was continuously employed in going to and fro between Northbourne and East Hagbourne with chisels to be sharpened for the shaping of the stone.

A foundation stone was laid by Mrs Bowles on Thursday 7 November 1889. The church was formally opened on 30 June 1890, by the Lord Bishop of Reading.

In 1897, there was a gale. The wind tore away the sheets of corrugated iron which for seven years had made a temporary roof for the tower portion of the church. A note was sent to the Revd Baker, who came across at once. He regarded the damage as a message; a committee was formed and set to work. A list of all the shareholders of the GWR was obtained, and each was written to, requesting that 1*s*. be given to the appeal. As a result the tower was added.

In the grounds of the church (now the Northbourne Centre) there is a very tall Wellingtonia fir tree; known just after the last war as the 'Christmas tree'. The tree originally was brought from Lockinge by Mr William Lewthwaite who had been a gardener to Lord Wantage.

St Peter's Church.

It was then a tiny tree that never did well at Lockinge; when transplanted at Didcot, it took off. This was about 1890. It was again transplanted into the grounds of St Peter's Church, in 1903, to celebrate the coronation year of Edward VII.

When the church was first opened, Northbourne was part of the ecclesiastical parish of East Hagbourne; it was not until 1915 that a separate parish of St Peter's was established. Up to that time curates from St Andrew's gave the services at St Peter's. Before the building of the parsonage in 1907, the curates used to live in lodgings in Northbourne.

The first school in Northbourne was established 1871, for infants alone. It was followed in 1874 by a mixed school for older children. Both were church schools, as is their successor of today. The old school in Northbourne was opened in 1877, enlarged in 1892, and again in 1894. There was a succession of masters during the period up to when the formidable George H. McFarlane was appointed in about 1894.

At the end of the nineteenth century, there was a proliferation of small shops in Northbourne. Their number seems far greater than the needs of that small community, but they did also cater for Didcot and East Hagbourne. Two of these shops were built quite early on,

Andrews at the top of the Hagbourne Road, and the off-licence in Church Street, both in 1870. Bosleys the butchers in Wallingford Road (or 65 Broadway) was built in 1873. Others followed: William Button in East Street, in 1880; John Fulford in High Street (lately Livings), 1881; John Pryor, lower Wallingford Road, 1890; Richard Edwards (or Dales) in High Street, 1891; and Andrews' other shop in Hagbourne Road in 1906. There was another shop, in Highfield House; in about 1908 it was a chemist's shop, run by a Mr Cowling. There was a great scandal when he committed suicide that year.

There were even more shops, but these were mainly the front-parlour type. There was a fish shop, and a hairdresser, both in Church Street. Joseph Bull, a shoemaker and repairer, also had a shop in High Street. The commercial directories for the late nineteenth century show that in 1883 there was a draper, three grocers and two beer retailers; the latter, the Railway Arms and the shop in

High Street in 1929. Dale's old shop was opened by the Edwards family in 1891. The cottages just beyond the shop, built in 1870, were demolished just after the Second World War.

Church Street (the off-licence). In 1887, there were two dressmakers, and even a toy shop. The toy shop lasted for some twenty years. Stephen Dixon's son, John, traded as a carpenter, upholsterer, cabinet maker and, later, as an undertaker.

The sheer number of these shops does show how relatively wealthy Northbourne was, when compared to the Didcot or East Hagbourne villages. There were more shops at Northbourne than there were at Harwell or Blewbury. That a toy shop was able to trade for over twenty years shows that there was money to be spent on more than basic needs, that there was room for luxury items; though presumably customers would come from afar to buy toys for their children.

Today, Northbourne's public house is the Sprat in Hagbourne Road. It was built by Messrs Pittman in 1879–80 and named the 'Railway Arms'; the first publican was a Jonathan Painter. He was followed by Fred Annette (1887), and by Charles Newman, who continued as landlord well into this century. It got its present name through colloquial use. It is said that railwaymen, when in the pub

The Sprat in Hagbourne Road. Originally known as the Railwaymen's Arms, which was built in 1879–80.

after work, would toast sprats over the pub fire for their tea; eventually, the pub was generally referred to as 'the Sprat', so the name was changed. But this did not occur until well into this century, until after the last war.

Northbourne was never extended outwards beyond the line of its outer streets, of West Street, South Street and beyond the Didcot–Newbury–Southampton Railway, before the Great War. One of the reasons was that Dixon did not own the land beyond West Street or Mereland Road in the west, and the railway line (of the Didcot–Southampton Railway) in the east (which was owned by more traditional landowners), but the land to the south beyond South Street or Wessex Road was his. The reason for not extending beyond the line of Wessex Road was that after 1895 he no longer owned this land.

The mortgage he had arranged originally back in 1868 was still outstanding in 1895. He never really managed to discharge any part of the debt. In 1880, with £3,775 still outstanding, Dixon paid off £50, and promptly borrowed another £150. Then in 1895, the patience of the remaining mortgagor, Edmund Ormond, being exhausted, he foreclosed, forcing Dixon to sell the remaining 89 acres of farmland still left over from the 123 acres purchased earlier in 1866. This land lay to the south of Wessex Road. The land was then conveyed to Ormond, which finally discharged Dixon's debts to the former. This 15 acres, the land on which Northbourne stands, a greater part of which had already been sold, was reconveyed to Dixon. The subsequent purchasers of the 89 acres were Robert Rich (25 acres), the Didcot–Southampton Railway Co., and Dennis Napper (44 acres).

Dixon died intestate the next year, the remaining estate passing to his heir Stephen Dixon, who died without issue in 1900, leaving his brother, John, as the next heir. John Dixon, one of Northbourne's more prominent residents at the end of the nineteenth century, was a carpenter, joiner and undertaker.

Obviously, one can only make surmises about Stephen Dixon. He must have been a very poor farmer, and an equally poor businessman, if he was unable to pay off his debts with the income coming in from the farms and the cottage rents, plus the money he got from selling land at Northbourne. If one compares him to Robert Rich or Dennis Napper, both of whom by the time of their deaths were practically millionaires, in value of properties owned, the difference is very apparent; and both were near contemporaries.

However, in all probability, the main reason for the failure to expand Northbourne in the late 1880s and '90s was that the housing famine of earlier decades had finally been satisfied. It has been said that at the turn of the century, and before the Great War, it was easy to rent, and that houses stood empty awaiting a tenant.

Northbourne was just not streets and houses, it was also people. It was to satisfy their housing needs that New Town was built.

Like any other place, it had its prominent people. The history of Stephen Dixon and Northbourne has already been given, but the most outstanding man of the time was undoubtedly Robert Rich, or 'Bobby' Rich, after whom Richmere Road and Rich's Sidings are named; and it is he, of all the people who have lived in Didcot during the past century, who is remembered most today, having left an indelible memory in the minds of those who knew him – even though he died over fifty years ago.

Rich was an enigmatic man, one who could be quite aloof at times though always polite; hence around him grew, inadvertently, an air

Robert Rich, 1855–1937.

of mystery. Myths were certainly created about him. Moreover, children of the period were always wary of him, keeping out of his way if they could, especially if previously caught trespassing on his land, which always made him angry. Sergeant Perry, the local policeman, another well-remembered man, would often be sent to call on the fathers of erring offspring, telling them to point out forcibly the error of their ways with a belt. This once happened to Walter Davies.

Rich was an unusual man: clever, highly intelligent, well educated and generous. He was respected by many in Old Didcot and Northbourne; and most people were simply in awe of him. The fact that he was the Chairman of the Magistrates added to his reputation. He acquired a great deal of land throughout his life and with other ventures grew very rich, which caused resentment in certain quarters – in Northbourne, in particular. In the period before the First World War, not being a farmer or railwayman, he bestrode the gap between the two communities of Old Didcot and Northbourne, being in neither camp.

Physically, he was a slim, wiry man of middle height, usually dressed in knickerbockers and gaiters, etc. He is also remembered for his very distinctive mustache.

His was a remarkable history. He was born in 1855 to a large family, with two brothers and five sisters. His father was Edmund Rich of Wollesley, near Malmesbury, land agent to a large estate in the West Country. He attended Bradfield College and, in 1871, the Royal Agricultural College at Cirencester where he had a brilliant academic and athletic career. In 1876, he was elected a Fellow of the Chartered Surveyors' Institute.

His first post was as resident agent to the 13,000 acre estate of the Earl of Ducie at Sarsden in North Oxfordshire. He was the youngest man in Britain to hold such a post. He was 21 years old.

In 1882, he became agent for Lord Wantage but left a year later for a comprehensive tour of the USA and Canada to study the cattle industry. After his return he became actively involved in liberal politics. Then in 1884, he went to Paris to become a lecturer at the Sorbonne. The next year, he was appointed Professor of Forestry and Agriculture at a new college established on the Earl of Cranborne's estate in Kent. Finally, he arrived in Didcot in August 1888, where he stayed until his death in 1937.

Something happened during his period with Lord Wantage that altered his whole life, so much so that he never achieved his full potential, even though he became very rich. His relationship with Lord Wantage had a very bitter quality.

He set up office – presumably as a surveyor – next to the entrance of what is now Rich's Sidings. Rich quickly established himself in Northbourne, gaining a reputation for kindness and generosity – in particular, he was very kind to a young widow who had been left destitute after her husband had been killed on the railway.

As mentioned previously, he designed and built St Peter's Church in 1891; and in the same year took upon himself the role of the railwaymen's champion in the great battle with Lord Wantage and the Revd William Baker over the establishment of a board school at Northbourne.

In 1899, he purchased John Blagrave's farm, or 'Blagraves' Farm', although it was known locally as 'Perrys' Farm', after the tenant at that time. Ownership of that farm gave Rich control of all the fields that ran up from lower Lydalls Road to the Broadway, from Edinburgh Drive eastward down to the lower Broadway. In time this

George McFarlane, the redoubtable headmaster of Northbourne School.

land became very valuable – on it is now sited the larger part of Didcot's shopping centre.

That experience with Lord Wantage turned him into a 'red hot radical'; preaching by platform and pen against the evils of 'squirearchy' and landlordism – the episode in 1891 shows exactly how he felt about Lord Wantage. It is a paradox in his own character that he spent the rest of his life buying and developing land, thus becoming a landlord in his own right. One of his last acts was supervising the building of 'Boots Corner' – the row of shops at the corner of Broadway–Station Road – in 1936.

It could be said that the period produced three outstanding men; Robert Rich was the first, another was Dennis Napper of Manor Farm, Old Didcot and the third, George R. McFarlane, the formidable headmaster of Northbourne School, who was appointed *c.* 1894. He was headmaster at Northbourne until his retirement in 1932. Many who went to Northbourne School during his time still remember him with respect and affection.

He was a legendary man, especially in the teaching profession – and to his former pupils, to whom he was known behind his back as 'Mac'. He commanded an enormous amount of respect from both these former pupils and the community at large, especially at Northbourne before the Great War. The tales told of him are many.

McFarlane was a stern, even fierce disciplinarian who died in 1951, at the age of 84. His obituary in the *Didcot Advertizer* of November 1951 stated that

> Didcot [had] lost one of its outstanding characters . . . news of his death was received with genuine sorrow by hundreds of ex-pupils who had known him since their childhood, and whom he still addressed by their christian names despite their adult status. He came from Culham Training College to be headmaster of what was then known as the North Hagbourne School; from which he retired at the age of 65, in 1932. A disciplinarian who was able to obtain obedience with the minimum of effort, [he] was not a believer in sparing the rod, thus gaining the healthy respect of his pupils. And though Mr. McFarlane might cane for the slightest infraction of the rules or even for mistakes in school work he was still held in great affection by those same pupils in later years. He knew all his children by christian names, even when middle-aged. It was said of him that his authority extended far beyond the school, and the sight of him in any part of the parish had a

restraining effect equal to that of two policemen. But he was a good teacher; and it was commonly said of him that if there was any good in a child, Mr. McFarlane would bring it out.

After his retirement, he was always available for advice and help, as many families of the period could attest. His funeral at East Hagbourne was attended by a bus load of former pupils and many others from the town.

S. Allen Warner wrote of him, or 'G.R.M.', as he was known affectionately, that he became a trainer of teachers, especially from Culham College, where he had been trained himself; and it was a common sight in the 1920s and '30s to see student teachers making their way from the station every morning to Mr McFarlane's school in Church Street.

Lesser contemporaries of Rich and McFarlane at the end of the century, and before the Great War, were John Dixon, Stephen Dixon's younger son; Thomas Andrews, and Alfred Bosley, butchers; Joseph Edenborough, diaryman; Richard Edwards, draper (Dales); Charles Newman of the Railway Arms; John Pryor, grocer; Raymond Ryman, fruiterer; these names come from a Kelly's Directory of 1903. Probably, of all these tradesman, the name of John Fulford will be most remembered. He was a grocer, and his shop was in High Street, now Livings. He was a prominent liberal, but is also remembered for being a hen-pecked husband.

Obviously, Old Didcot and Northbourne at the turn of the century had produced some giants; and their like will not be repeated because conditions in Didcot today are so very different.

4

Life at North Hagbourne, with Robert Rich, 1870–1900

In 1977, members of the Didcot Archaeological Society visited Mrs Grace Smith at her home in High Street, Northbourne, which is now just a suburb of a wider Didcot, to question her about her childhood at the end of the nineteenth century in what was then Didcot Newtown. She was born in 1894 and moved to Northbourne soon after her birth. She lived first in Wallingford Road, then East Street, and later High Street.

She remembers what was for her a golden childhood, in those last few years of the Victorian era before the outbreak of the Great War: her parents, Nathaniel and Sarah Belcher, her neighbours and the small enclosed world of Didcot Newtown. Her memories of that period are of dusty roads in summer, muddy roads in winter, of Wallingford Road as 'the top road' and Wessex Road as the 'bottom road'; of scattering ashes on the muddy surface of High Street in winter, of standing in thick mud outside Dales; of childhood games, hopscotch, whip and top, and marbles. She remembered those early years with great affection. As did the late Mr Walter Davies of Old Didcot. He had similar, very happy memories of his childhood, though his family was poor, in the village just before 1914.

Obviously, in old age, childhood memories come back with great clarity, but they do end up rosy tinged, with all negative elements generally wiped away. It was not quite as rosy as they remembered.

Living conditions for the working classes in these new cottages, both at Old Didcot and Northbourne, during the last three decades of the nineteenth century, could be and were very poor, due to bad

High Street, c. *1898.*

sanitation and drainage, and from the refusal of landlords to make essential improvements. It took members of the Wallingford Rural District Council well over twenty years to achieve a situation where those in Newtown had clean water piped into their homes, plus proper sewers, with the result that they were free from disease. But it was a battle, with the landlords fighting a rearguard action all the way back to their banks.

The minutes of the Sanitary Authority chart the history of this conflict. The earliest minute records the visit of the Sanitary Inspector, in July 1878, who reported 'the existence of a nuisance at East Hagbourne arising from the foul and offensive nature of the privvies and cess pits belonging to dwelling houses situate in a new street, North Hagbourne . . .'. While another minute a month later reports that 'the drainage from the cottages at North Hagbourne, passes into an open ditch by the side of the road, at the Hagbourne (toll) gate and thereby causes a nuisance'. These cottages are the long terraces at the end of Church Street. Later in 1893, a Mr F.E. Hunt of Newtown Terrace (29–41 Broadway), wrote to the RDC complaining about the foul condition of the same ditch – fifteen years

An early postcard of the lower Broadway, looking west, c. *1905.*
(Don Farnborough)

later. Then again, in 1880, the Sanitary Inspector reported on the defective conditions of the drainage 'of the newly erected group of houses situated at East Hagbourne Newtown', despite repeated requests to Stephen Dixon and other landlords that improvements be made. They continued to ignore abatement orders, and the foul conditions, especially ditches, still full of rubbish and sewage, remained unchanged. Then Newtown was visited by the Medical Officer of Health; and his report of February 1882 is very revealing as to the state of the houses and cottages of Northbourne at that time:

> that in a recent inspection which I made in company with the Sanitary Inspector, of Didcot Newtown, my attention was directed to the very unsatisfactory character of the new cottages so many of which are in the course of erection there, and . . . the time has come when it is most desirable in the interests of public health and even in that of the owners of such property that you should make application for such limited urban powers as would enable you to make byelaws to the erection of new buildings in this locality. The Census returns [show] that the population of East Hagbourne which was in 1871, 798 persons living in 190 houses had in 1881

> increased to 1108 occupying 231 houses, consequently the density of population per house had increased in ten years from 4.2 to 4.8. House building is now going on to a considerable extent but on inspection of the new buildings I found a great deficiency of such essential requisites of a healthy dwelling as sufficient area of site, proper thickness of walls, wholesome appliances and arrangements and even due security against fire. As regards drainage and sewage disposal, the ordinary cesspool is almost universal and in such small plots of land as are allowed to these cottages, cesspools cannot fail in a short space of time to foul the drinking water and . . . I remind you of the outbreaks of preventive disease that have occurred in this part of your district within the last few years traceable to this cause and very recently I have had under examination water samples from cottages here where the tenements were really of a superior character but the water had become dangerous and even effusively foul from the bad system of drainage adopted. As matters now stand, you are without powers to interfere until a nuisance has actually been created. Should you however determine to apply for urban powers . . .

What the doctor's inspection had revealed was that in these small back gardens both wells and cesspools were in close proximity, so that drinking water was generally fouled by the seepage of sewage. Water when taken for testing was often found to be brown in colour. Consequently, there was in those years a high incidence of contagious diseases, such as tuberculosis, enteric fever, puerperal fever, scarlet fever, diphtheria, and even, at times, typhoid. There were one or two cases of smallpox.

The members of the authority during this early period were so worried about the widespread incidence of disease that they did all in their power to eradicate it, so much so that by the turn of the century conditions had improved dramatically, though this is not to say that outbreaks of disease had been completely eliminated. People did live in filthy conditions, a breeding ground for disease, which were often created by themselves; and bad housing was still outside the jurisdiction of the local authority.

It is not generally realized what a great debt we owe to these early councillors. Though the social gulf between them and that working class population was large, these middle-class councillors did what they did because it was their duty; even though they all thought Northbourne to be an ugly intrusion into the rural landscape.

After receiving the Medical Officer of Health's damning report, the Wallingford Sanitary Authority did apply to the Local Government Board for powers to make model bye-laws as was recommended: the request was granted and these came into force, November 1882.

The adoption of these bye-laws may, possibly, have been another factor in the decline of house building at Northbourne during the 1880s. The model bye-laws controlled the construction of all future buildings, and demanded that houses be properly constructed, with regard to fire prevention and the provision of correct sanitary facilities. Prospective builders now had to submit detailed building plans for approval – which were often rejected – before building could take place. Obviously, this made house building more expensive, and probably did affect future development. It is noticeable how house building slowed down after the bye-laws were adopted, though the major factor for this lack of growth was still the slackening of demand for housing. The bye-laws also applied to the streets as well as to the houses.

In February 1883, The Sanitary Authority applied to make Northbourne a Special Drainage District, under the Public Health Act 1875. If granted, the Special Drainage District would therefore

Wessex Road about 1910. The row of cottages, those in the middle foreground now demolished, were built by the GWR in c. *1907.*

(Don Farnborough)

exist 'for the purpose of charging thereon exclusively the expenses of work of sewerage, which by the Public Health Act, 1975, . . . may be declared special expenses'. No wonder the landlords and other ratepayers fought this proposal, for it meant that all expenses would be chargeable on the rates – those that existed at that time – and payable exclusively by the ratepayers of Didcot and Northbourne.

After several years of negotiations involving the Local Government Board with Stephen Dixon, other landlords and the Revd W.R. Baker (vicar of East Hagbourne, who was concerned about the bad conditions at Northbourne), an inquiry was held, December 1885. At which, the authority's application was refused, on the grounds of insufficient need. This left the authority in an impossible situation: unable to improve conditions by putting down sewers, or providing clean water, as they could not charge the district for the expense – to the relief, no doubt, of ratepayers spared heavy rate bills.

But the Local Government Board still continued to write pointing out the conditions at Northbourne. The clerk replied that as the board had failed to approve their application, nothing else could be done, other than press the landlords to abate the nuisance. The authority was then assailed from other points. The Thames Conservancy complained about sewage fouling the Thames, via polluted ditches and Moor Ditch; and reports were still being received about polluted water, ditches and of outbreaks of disease. In October 1889, 'to a case of enteric fever at North Hagbourne in a house occupied by Powell, a railway signalman. Well to be thoroughly cleaned.' There the situation rested, though there was continual debate during the years leading up to 1895, and the creation in that year of the Wallingford Rural District Council. Earlier in 1894, the authority had appointed an engineer, Mr Baldwin Latham, to prepare a plan for the drainage of Northbourne. As can be imagined, the owners and ratepayers thought his plan too expensive, and appointed their own engineer to prepare an alternative scheme. The board wrote asking about the present position. The clerk replied that the owners' engineer had estimated that the cost of the scheme would not be less than £5,000; and that the proposed site (just north-west of Cow Lane; Didcot sewage works was there until the late 1960s) was at present under water (November 1894); he further stated that as the Sanitary Authority was soon to go out of existence, the system best be left to the new Rural District Council for a decision.

The first meeting of the new authority was on 8 January 1895; and it received an abatement order from the Thames Conservancy, to cease the discharge of sewage into the Thames within three months – an order which could not possibly be obeyed.

As it was the most pressing problem facing the new council, a committee was formed. It recommended that Mr Latham's scheme be adopted, and that his plans be submitted to the Local Government Board; the estimated cost of the Special Drainage District was to be £6,670; and negotiations were opened with Lord Wantage to buy land north of the railway for the sewage works. There were still objections: this time from the East Hagbourne Parish Council. In August, the council applied to the Local Government Board for another inquiry, which was held January 1896. This time the council was successful; and work was set in progress. Over the next year, the costs of the scheme were discussed; land purchased, sewers slowly laid throughout the district, and the sewage works opened August 1898. Thereafter, all buildings, schools, houses, were slowly connected to the system. It was not until after 1900, that the council began piping water into every building within the Special Drainage District, and this was still being done as late as 1906. Northbourne wells were inspected in October 1905; and where householders were still relying on wells, the water generally was polluted; in many cases 'the water was more or less tinged, and in some to have a slight smell'.

But disease had not been completely eliminated. There were some bad outbreaks of scarlet fever and diphtheria among children attending school in the 1900s. At Didcot, the local school had to close on three separate occasions in January 1912, owing to the spread of scarlet fever, diphtheria and measles. In the following month, the infection spread to the Northbourne school, which also had to close.

Roads were another problem for the new council, especially secondary roads. They were either dusty in summer, or impassable, with mud and continual flooding preventing passage in winter. In Northbourne, Didcot and, for that matter, the rest of the district, the council tried to maintain good roads, but it proved very difficult to keep to the standards set. The roads were generally surfaced with granite or some similar stone, which was flattened by steam rollers, but the passage of large wooden-wheeled vehicles, farm wagons, etc., tended to break up this surface so that continual repairs were needed, and at great expense. Winter conditions were another factor, when floods, snow, ice and slush also accelerated the surface damage. The problem was eventually solved in the 1920s.

Culturally, the villages and Northbourne were centuries apart. Old Didcot and East Hagbourne were still set in a pre-industrial world which had its origins in the Middle Ages. Their allegiance was owed to squire and parson. The railwaymen, if they had an allegiance, owed it to the directors of the Great Western Railway Company, its senior officers – and to any influential traveller they might encounter. In one way, of course, their attitudes were similar: both groups had to be deferential just to keep their jobs, and their homes. But there the similarity ended. The railwaymen were living in the modern world, the villagers were not. The latter were still subject to the wishes of the parson and even to the arbitrary whims of their employers, the farmers. Step out of line, and they could easily lose their jobs, their homes, be thrown off the parish and forced into the workhouse. Poverty was the dreadful threat, and incarceration in the workhouse the nightmare. Subservience, touching the forelock, had to be the order of the day for them. Mr Walter Davies in his memoirs recorded how his mother and the other village women would curtsey as the Rector passed by; this was just before the First World War.

The railwaymen, by contrast, when work was done, were free of this form of feudalism. They owed respect to no one when at home. Ernest Simmons, in his *Memoirs of a Stationmaster*, writes of his battles with the company's hierarchy. He even challenged – if he is to be believed – Mr Peach, the stationmaster, to a fight, when unjustly accused; and the rest of the many employees at the station were equally disrespectful, but only behind his back. They were fiercely independent, and resented the almost feudalistic regime to which the villagers were subjected. In 1891, even Lord Wantage, that powerful aristocrat, was firmly put in what the railwaymen thought was his place. Lord Wantage was a kind, thoughtful employer, unusual for his time, but he was paternalistic. He did expect his inferiors to do as they were told without question.

Another reason for this relative independence was that they were well paid. It has already been noted that in 1861, one railway porter could afford a female servant. Their wages, which for a porter might not be that great, were paid regularly: it was not always so for a village labourer. The many shops – even that toy shop – in Northbourne in the 1880s, showed just how prosperous they were in relation to those in the villages. In the same period, Old Didcot and East Hagbourne had relatively few shops, certainly not of the range provided at Northbourne.

Politically, when compared to the villagers, the railwaymen were highly sophisticated. It was pointed out by one newcomer to Didcot, who came here as late as 1914, that many Didcot parish councillors could not read, and resisted any changes that were suggested by the railwaymen. It may seem hard to believe now that in 1914 some villagers, even parish councillors, could not read; but remember that compulsory education did not come in until 1870, and even afterwards many villagers were so poor that they could not afford to let their children go to school after the age of 10, sending them out to earn a living.

For these many reasons the railwaymen were disliked, even hated, by many, if not all, in the villages around. This dislike extended through all classes, from the lowliest villager to the parsons of Didcot and East Hagbourne, the Revd John Brown and the Revd W.R. Baker. This feeling between the latter and the railwaymen of Northbourne was bitterly mutual. The great battle between Northbourne and Lord Wantage in 1891 (see pp. 67–9) over the board school, was partly due to the unwelcome attentions of the Revd W.R. Baker. He was heartily disliked. The attitudes of these two clerics can be understood easily; simply, they did not receive from the railwaymen the almost sycophantic respect given to them by those in the two villages.

It is really hard to understand the feelings that were generated by these intense emotions such a long time ago; and to say that these hatreds were still felt until very recently is even harder to understand. It is only now, however, that these attitudes and emotions are disappearing from those people who, during that time as children inherited the hatreds of their parents, and who are now dying out themselves. Mr Walter Davies, who as a boy, living in Old Didcot between 1901 and 1912, when asked in 1977 about Northbourne during those years replied, 'I know nothing about Newtown. We had nothing to do with them.' He would not talk about Northbourne. Those feelings were shared by many in the 1960s and '70s.

These attitudes toward Northbourne were also shared by every visitor who came to Didcot, starting with those middle-class councillors of the Wallingford Rural District Council at the turn of the century. Their collective attitude was one of distaste for what they considered to be a squalid collection of cottages and houses: an ugly intrusion into the rural landscape.

This attitude was shared by more than one travel writer who came to Didcot for the railway. They thought Old Didcot with its little church reasonably attractive, and always enthused about the charms of East Hagbourne, but described Northbourne as an abomination. One writer suggested it be razed to the ground. But J.E. Vincent, in his *Highways and Byways of Berkshire* (1911), really went overboard when he wrote of Northbourne,

> except for some of the mining villages of South Wales, there are few aggregations of houses so bare and depressing as Didcot . . . and the scenery of Didcot is as dreary and monotonous as are its rows of uncompromising cottages all of one class, and all of a modern date. But . . . Didcot is not likely to become a popular resort, mainly because it is so ugly . . .

And he continues in a similar vein, saying Didcot 'is not a residential neighbourhood', and you could not live there.

It could be considered that these comments are rather harsh: Northbourne was never as bad as that description might suggest. But there is no doubt that to these professional travellers of pre-1914, Northbourne was an ugly sight. It must have been rare to find, and see, an urban development stuck out in the middle of nowhere; and it was just as Vincent described it, row after row of these ugly cottages, of no particular architectural merit, built by jobbing builders to their own designs, and surrounded by a dreary flat landscape that stretched for miles. No trees other than those that lined the Wallingford–Wantage Road. It must have been this contrast of streets of cottages against this flat landscape that made Northbourne look so drab, especially so in winter. This can be seen in some postcards of the period.

Not all railwaymen lived in Northbourne. As previously shown, there was a sizeable minority living in Old Didcot: in 1861, this was 39.54 per cent. In East Hagbourne in 1881 there were about ten families, though many from the two villages had migrated to Northbourne when houses became available for rent, from 1868 onwards.

But it was the railwaymen who dominated the politics of East Hagbourne before the First World War. A paradox really, when the population of East Hagbourne was much greater than that of Northbourne. The first poll for the East Hagbourne Parish Council, set up under the Local Government Act 1894, was held at Northbourne schoolroom, 4 December 1894. This may be the very reason why at each election the majority of parish councillors elected came from Northbourne. Presumably, most of the voters, who in the main were labourers or servants from East Hagbourne, could not be bothered to walk to Northbourne to vote, or did not want to go there. What we do not know is why Northbourne's schoolroom was chosen for each election, when there were facilities equally as good at East Hagbourne – in their own school. The election was called by the two overseers of the poor, who may possibly have been Northbourne residents.

At the first poll twenty-two candidates put their names forward, and on a show of hands nine were elected. William White, an East Hagbourne voter, demanded a poll. This was held 17 December, and those elected were: James Pether, 115 votes, bricklayer, EH; John Fulford, 107 votes, grocer, NB; John Hobbs, 107 votes, coal agent, NB; James R. Wood, 107 votes, builder, NB; Thomas Day, 99 votes, railway inspector, NB; Alfred Woodley, 96 votes, labourer, EH; Thomas Smith, 92 votes, engine driver, NB; Alfred Dearlove, 80 votes, labourer, EH; John T. Slade, 77 votes, railway labourer, EH; and James Lavell, of East Street, Northbourne, was elected Chairman.

There was tremendous interest shown in this first election, as can be seen from the number of votes cast – 1,284, or 875 for those successful, and 409 for the losers; and from those who had put themselves forward from East Hagbourne, and had been elected. This must have been a busy day for Northbourne, with over five hundred people milling around, moving to and fro, outside the schoolroom in Church Street.

This was not the case in subsequent elections, as shown in that for 1897, when of the nine councillors elected, eight came from Northbourne: Thomas Day, railway inspector, NB; Joseph Edenborough, dairyman, NB; John Fulford, grocer, NB; Thomas French, railway signalman, NB; Alfred Luker, insurance agent, NB; Albert Loveday, blacksmith, NB; Isaac Napper, butcher, EH; Edward Taylor, railway guard, NB; and Alfred Woodley, platelayer, EH; the Chairman was still John Lavell of Northbourne. This time the votes recorded for each candidate were very low.

In the 1907 election, the most votes (21) recorded were for George McFarlane, the Northbourne School headmaster. Certainly, after that first election year the novelty had worn off: and it had been the first time that so many, in particular, labourers from East Hagbourne, had been able to vote – the vote had been granted to agricultural labourers in 1885.

A similar election had taken place in Old Didcot, on 17 December 1894; and there the old order was firmly in control: John Brown, the Rector, was elected Chairman, and the councillors (farmers all), were, William Napper, Henry Smith, Dennis Napper, George C. Hobbs and Alfred Campbell.

It was politics that brought about the conflict between Rich and Lord Wantage over the board school, in 1891.

The first school to be established at Northbourne was a church school, which was opened in 1871, for infants only. Later, in 1891, there was still just the infants school; Miss Fanny Chapman, mistress. The older children had to walk across the fields to attend East Hagbourne's church school, which was very firmly under the control of the Revd William Baker, as was the infants school in Northbourne.

It was in 1891 that the demand grew in Northbourne for a board school, or an elementary school, controlled not by the Church as at East Hagbourne, but by a school board, a locally elected body, who would be able to levy rates to pay for it. The Education Act 1870 stated that board schools were to be established in areas where efficient church schools were not already in place. Northbourne fitted this bill.

The battle for the board school was one that was many-faceted. On one side, it was rearguard action by ratepayers wishing to avoid the imposition of another rate; on another, it was the established Church against the nonconformists, of which, as Rich himself said, over half the population of Northbourne were; these were some of the reasons for the involvement of many who were anti-board school. There was also that anti-railwayman feeling that was so very strong in the area around Northbourne; a movement led by the Revd Baker and other clerics. It could be said that Lord Wantage shared these attitudes. He had, in late 1889, called railwaymen 'mules', which did not go down very well. The intervention of Lord Wantage added an extra dimension. It was not only a philosophical battle between the old order and the new, between Lord Wantage, the Revd Baker and their Church Party and the railwaymen. It also became a personal battle between Lord Wantage and Robert Rich.

It was an extension, a renewal of a personal battle which the two had had, when Rich was in Lord Wantage's employment in 1882–3. Had it not been for Lord Wantage's involvement, the poll would have been won, and today, Northbourne School, as a church school, would not exist. But he was determined to get his own way.

For reasons unknown, a substantial nonconformist group began the agitation for a board school. Notices, headed 'Board School or Parson's School', were put up around Northbourne, to advertise a meeting that was held 'in Mr. Fulford's Meadow', 14 June 1891.

The decision of this public meeting, presumably, was to carry on the campaign, which came to a head at a parish meeting on 12 October. The London newspaper, *The Star*, reported the meeting under its headline, 'Plain words to a Peer'; the news item made it clear that the railwaymen were not going to be ruled by the old order, by squire or parson. The Revd Baker tried to take the chair, but he was soon voted down. A vote was taken, and carried, that a school board be formed.

It was just after the vote, that Lord Wantage entered the room, his carriage having broken down. After some discussion, Robert Rich rose to address the meeting, when Lord Wantage, said somewhat curtly and pointedly, 'You must wait till the chairman has done.' To which, Rich cried passionately,

> I will not be put down by you. I have had enough of your tyranny. Eight years ago you tried your worst to take away my daily bread by the vilest, most unjust, most dishonourable and most dastardly lying means that any creature of your kind could conceive. But you shall not silence me now. I will speak in spite of you and your peerage.

Lord Wantage's response to this outburst was to say nothing, so after a painful pause the motion that a poll be held was carried, and the meeting was then adjourned abruptly.

A week later, the Church Party, under the chairmanship of the Revd Baker, held a meeting in the schoolroom at Northbourne, which forty members of the opposition tried to attend, only to be met at the door by the vicar, who told them they were not wanted, and to leave. They had come from East Hagbourne, and on returning to the village, were abused and threatened as they walked down the village street. The majority of the villagers, and all the public houses, especially, were supporters of the vicar.

The school board held their last meeting in Robert Rich's shed on 25 October, the day before that of the poll; it was presided over by Major Pilcher, of East Hagbourne.

Rich, in his address to the meeting, accused the stationmaster of currying favour with Baker and Lord Wantage; and that 'some of those GWR platform men, who always rush up to the first class carriages, and away from the poverty-stricken thirds, are also signing this billet-doux . . .' – a petition set up by the stationmaster rallying support for Lord Wantage.

The poll was held Monday 26 October 1891. Lord Wantage had told his tenants at East Hagbourne to bring themselves and their labourers across to Northbourne, to vote against the motion. The *Bucks and Oxon Advertizer* reported the scene:

> Posters were freely posted about the parish in favour of the Board, and handbills delivered to every house, and from one end of the district to the other there was as much excitement as at a general election. By a coincidence, of course, Lord Wantage's rent audit was being held at East Hagbourne . . . and Lord Wantage himself appeared early to vote against the Board.

Two great wagon loads of labourers were brought across to record their vote.

It was a foregone conclusion. Lord Wantage and the Revd Baker won the day. The former did as he had promised, to enlarge the school at Northbourne, which was done in 1892, to accommodate about two hundred children, all those from Northbourne; and George R. McFarlane was appointed headmaster. Lord Wantage also promised to pay his salary of £140 p.a., which he did. Northbourne never did get its board school, and never again was there any agitation for it, but the community did get Mr McFarlane, who was his own man and not the vicar's; so it could be said that it was a draw.

The railwaymen and his other supporters, such as Major Pilcher of East Hagbourne, were determined to show Robert Rich their appreciation and in January 1892 the whole of Northbourne turned out and in a long procession carried him in triumph down Station Hill to the Corn Exchange. There he was fêted, speeches were made and he was given an illuminated address and two walking sticks.

5

An Eventful Seven Years, 1879–1886

The seven years that ran from 1879 to 1886 witnessed a number of events that were important at the time – although not today; they were, the dissolution of the Wallingford–Faringdon Turnpike Trust in 1879; the construction of the Didcot–Newbury–Southampton Railway in 1882; the laying down of the railway west curve, and the demolishment of Foxhall House in 1884; the building of the Provender Store in 1885; and the great fire at Didcot Station in 1886.

The Wallingford–Faringdon Turnpike Road

Roads in the seventeenth and eighteenth centuries were generally awful. The best roads were still those laid down by the Romans, that were wide with hard surfaces – when they had survived. But the majority of roads were narrow, with soft surfaces. In summer, when at their best, the traveller was covered by clouds of dust; in winter, when no one travelled if it could be avoided, they were impassable, and were turned into deep quagmires, with enormous potholes. Consequently, travel under these conditions was impossible; and roads by the end of winter would end up being much wider than their actual width, as travellers in their vehicles tried to find a firmer surface. But this would only apply to roads bordering open fields where there were no restrictions – in the form of hedges or ditches – to access to the fields. At Didcot, for instance, the main road (today the Wantage Road–Broadway), was bordered on each side by drainage ditches, which did restrict wagons and carriages to the road proper; which became a long ribbon of liquid mud, churned up by each passing vehicle, and almost axle deep. Pity the poor horses. High Street, in Northbourne, was like this: at Edwards shop (or Dales), they had to put down wood faggots to help carts get up the slope.

Short journeys could take weeks; and apocryphal stories of travellers, horse and all, disappearing down into enormous potholes were legion. Because of the conditions, road traffic in winter was very light. It was easier to travel by horse. Consequently, trade was severely affected; and it was to remedy these deficiencies that the turnpike road system came into being. Tolls were levied on travellers and the money collected was used for the repair and upkeep of the roads. Eventually, the Turnpike Trusts were created, usually a body of local gentry, who would take over a stretch of road, build and install toll-houses and gates, and charge tolls, to be used to improve and maintain the roads. This was the theory; reality is always different. Many trusts were dishonest, inefficient, or negligent.

Therefore, it was these conditions – an impassable road – that led to the creation of the Wallingford–Faringdon Turnpike Road Trust, introduced by an Act of Parliament in 1752. The 'Gentlemen, Clergy and Freeholders of the Vale of the White Horse' petitioned parliament in that year, requesting that a turnpike trust be created to take over maintenance of this road. Their petition said of the Vale, that

> The same is an exceedingly rich and fertile Vale, of great Extent, both as to Length and Breadth, and producing annually Quantities of Corn, Butter and Cheese which for the Want of good Roads and Markets, are rendered almost useless to the Publick, and that the Farms are hereby impoverished, and Farmers very frequently ruined; but that the Petitioners apprehend, that in case a good Road be made through the Vale, and an easy Communication opened to the River of Thames, and Cities of London and Westminster, it must necessarily be productive of good Effects, not only to the Vale of Berkshire but many other parts of the Kingdom.

Their parliamentary Act was passed, and the turnpike trust set up. But we do not know how honest or efficient this trust was; did they provide a good road surface – especially as the turnpike gates were leased out for three years at a time? We do not know and never will.

This particular turnpike road ran from Faringdon to Wallingford,

The Star Inn or the Dirt House on the Wallingford Road; an inn that benefited from the passing trade on the turnpike road. *(Mrs Margaret Potter)*

and eventually on to Nuffield Common. Today, this is the A417–A4130. The A4130 branches off from the A417 at Harwell, continuing on to Didcot and Wallingford. The section of the road which ran through Didcot is now the Wantage Road –Broadway. The A417 continues on to Upton, Blewbury and then to Streatley. It too was turnpiked; there was a gate at the Scotland Ash Corner, by the Horse and Harrow public house, at West Hagbourne.

Originally, there were only four gates on the Wallingford–Faringdon Turnpike: the Stanford Gate (between Faringdon and Stanford-in-the-Vale); the Charlton Gate (at the village of Charlton, now absorbed into, and on the east side of, Wantage); the Ludbridge Gate (on the road between East and West Hendred, where Mill Brook passes under the road); and the Wallingford Gate (the west side of Wallingford). By 1844, a further gate had been established at Challow, the East Challow Gate. It replaced the Ludbridge Gate which was closed. The Wallingford Gate was also closed, and before 1844, it too was replaced, this time by the Slade End Gate.

Toll-houses and gates were built in places where they could levy tolls on vehicles going in and out, and through, the main towns of Faringdon, Wantage and Wallingford. It seems surprising that before 1840 there were no more than four gates. Their siting also seems somewhat odd. There were, for instance, no gates between Wallingford and East Hendred, and none on either side of Harwell. It is possible that there were other gates earlier in the eighteenth century abandoned as being uneconomic. There were still only the four in 1826; and they, when put out to tender, produced a sum in excess of £678 for the trustees. However, their numbers did increase at the beginning of the railway age.

The improvement, though gradual, to the road surface must have been of great benefit to the traveller. There are no records left from the turnpike days to assess its economic fortunes. One indirect way is to note the various inns erected to cater for the passing trade. Road improvements did mean an increasing number of road users. The Star Inn, or the Dirt House on the Wallingford Road, between Didcot and Wallingford; the old Wheatsheaf, formerly in the Wantage Road, Didcot; and the White Hart in Harwell; all benefited from passing travellers. However, all these inns, mainly sixteenth or seventeenth century in date, were already there when the trust was formed. Both the Wheatsheaf and the White Hart were enlarged in the late eighteenth century.

The opening of Didcot Junction in 1844 meant an increasing

amount of traffic going to the station; and with the consequent wearing of the road surface, the trustees responded by opening a new gate, 'the Didcot Gate' (it was also known locally as 'the Wheatsheaf Gate'), and building a small toll-house beside it in 1846. The toll-house was sited on the south side of Wantage Road, just to the west of the Foxhall Road junction. There was also a bar to Park Road, and there must have been another one immediately to the east of the junction (now the Broadway), outside the petrol station. The gates and bars meant that all traffic coming from the west and south would be charged tolls.

Another gate was opened a year or two after the establishment of the Didcot Corn Exchange in 1857. This gate, sited lower down the Broadway, and immediately to the east of the entrance to Rich's Sidings, was called 'the Hagbourne Gate'; and there was a bar to Hagbourne Road. Now all the traffic to the station and the Corn Exchange had to pay tolls.

The late Charles Lovelock when a boy of 5 years stayed once in the Didcot Gate toll-house. He left a description: 'the tollhouse was a

The Didcot Gate on the turnpike just beyond the Foxhall Road–Broadway crossroad, photographed about 1870. The lady is Bessie Lovelock, daughter of the toll collector of the time.

little single-story building, with side windows looking out up and down the road so as to obtain a good view of the passing traffic.'

The rate of tolls charged in the eighteenth century is not known; but in November 1859 an advertisement appeared in the *Reading Mercury*, advising road users that the toll for 'every horse and other beasts drawing any carriage, wagon, cart, etc.' would be increased from 4*d.* to 4½*d.* (roughly 2p); which by the monetary standards of the times was quite expensive.

The tolls were fiercely resented, and some stories have come down to us of the means used to avoid paying them. The Squire of Fulscot Manor used at times to jump horseback over the Hagbourne Gate in protest against the charges there levied. Another story concerns the enterprise of a man who took advantage of the regulation whereby anyone who had goods to sell in the village came in free of toll. He used to have some logs of wood in his cart, which he would leave behind him with a friend in the village when he had occasion to make his homeward journey. People entering or leaving the village had to pay at only one gate, and a pass was given when they entered from east or west, enabling them to leave by the alternate road without further charge.

Another story concerned a tollgate keeper, who got married on the strength of securing the job, and with his wife commenced housekeeping with nothing else than a bale of straw, some canvas and two boxes. Their wage was very small, but they had free lodgings and fuel, and in the course of some years they were able to retire, and live a life of leisure on their savings of several hundred pounds.

The end of the turnpike system was in sight when the trustees opened the Hagbourne Gate and Bar. The railways by taking over much of the transport of goods from the roads and canals had started the process of decay, when many trusts went bankrupt. The establishment of highway boards continued their decline. In this area it was Moreton Highway Board; it too went out of existence with the creation of the county councils in 1888, which took over responsibility for highways.

The Wallingford–Faringdon Turnpike Trust was finally dissolved in 1879–80. It had applied to parliament for a renewal of its powers in 1875, and an Act was passed, with an option to renew in 1878. The option was never taken up, and the trust was ended. The tollhouses and gates were removed, and very quickly, afterwards.

A train on the Didcot–Newbury–Southampton railway line passes by Fleet Meadow, now the site of the Fleetway housing estate. The caravan site would be on the left.

The Didcot–Newbury–Southampton Railway

The idea for this railway originated back in the 1840s when the first scheme was suggested, of a link between the industrial Midlands and Southampton and other southern ports. Other schemes were subsequently put forward, but they all came to nothing.

Another attempt was made in the 1870s, with the firmly held objectives of not only providing this link between the Midlands and Southampton, but also of giving a new service to a largely isolated agricultural community, in Berkshire and Hampshire. The national network would benefit by this new railway and at the same time provide fresh markets for the farmers in this area, who were experiencing declining prosperity. Thus, in 1873, a new company was launched, the Didcot, Newbury and Southampton Railway, which was incorporated by Act of parliament in August that year.

The scheme was heavily dependent on one vital factor, that the link between the southern ports and the industrial north be an overwhelming success. Without that there was no way that the area through which the line was to run, an area of small villages and hamlets, sparsely populated, of low productivity, and with little or no industry, could support a railway.

The company tried without success for several years to raise the necessary capital, until finally the promoter, a William Tatham, decided to introduce a Bill into parliament, so that he could abandon the line, and recover his deposit. It was at this point that some of the more important landowners, such as the Earl of Carnarvon, around Newbury, decided to intervene to save the line, by acquiring the company from Mr Tatham.

They, like many before them, had faith in the company's belief that there was a need for a rail link to the industrial north, and that it was a viable project; in that they were sadly mistaken and so were those who invested heavily in the company. This time the company was successful in attracting capital, through the eminence of those who constituted its board of directors: the Chairman was Colonel Sir Robert Loyd-Lindsay, VC, later Lord Wantage; other directors were equally eminent. It was their very names that attracted the necessary capital; and they were helped by Lord Carnarvon, and other local landowners from around Newbury. But one thing these eminent directors had in common – they knew nothing about railways; and because of this they always came off the worst in the their dealings with the GWR – the line was to start at the GWR's junction at Didcot.

A Newbury-bound train leaving the Didcot–Newbury–Southampton Railway platform bay at Didcot sometime after the First World War.

The line throughout its whole history was never profitable. This was partly due to the heavy capital costs of building the line originally. The railway was laid down through extremely difficult countryside – undulating downland, the great chalk slopes of the Berkshire and Hampshire Downs, which at their peak were 900 ft above sea level. This terrain demanded a large number of expensive cuttings, embankments and bridges. There were other factors that increased costs. Though it was at first a single-track line, this being sufficient for the local community, it was designed to take a double track, the bed was wide enough at 26 ft, to accommodate the increased traffic from the Midlands – if it should materialize. The GWR also demanded that it had to have easy gradients; and there was a need for fast curves to speed all that supposed traffic on to the southern ports. Compensation to greedy landowners also helped to increase these heavy costs.

The line was constructed in two sections, the first, the Newbury section, from Didcot to Newbury, the second, Newbury to Southampton. Work started on the northern section in 1879. In April 1881, the section of the line which passed through East Hagbourne (or Didcot, as it is now) was then being laid down. Some thirty labourers, and one of the contractors, were lodging in the village of East Hagbourne. The material that made up the extensive embankments which carried the line from Didcot Station across the fields at East Hagbourne came from the cuttings made at Upton.

Work proceeded slowly at first but was completed in April 1882. The line was opened Wednesday 12 April at Newbury, by the Mayor of Newbury. He and other civic dignitaries with many distinguished visitors took the train for Didcot, arriving there about 1 p.m. A large banner was hung, bearing the legend, 'Success to the DN & SR', welcoming this party. The line ran from a single platform constructed on the east end of the station, on the south side.

The railway was built with great expectations in mind; and they were not the only ones. At Didcot, in 1882, a company from Newbury, the Newbury Land and Building Company, also with great dreams of wealth to come, acquired 15 acres from Stephen Dixon, to speculate on the land boom which the company thought would soon materialize. Presumably, they knew of the earlier demand for houses in Northbourne, which the GWR line had created, and thought that the new railway would cause a similar demand. But they were mistaken.

The land they bought was that arc of land bordered on the west by

Hagbourne Road, on the east by the railway line, and on the north by the Wallingford Road. Today this land is occupied by the caravan site and the new housing estate, which in turn occupies the site of the former Jobs Dairy.

The company produced a plan to build on this land a large estate made up of 6 streets and 199 houses. Luckily for us, the plan never got beyond the planning stage: eventually the company went into liquidation, and the land was sold. However, it does seem that some of the houses were built: the terrace row of seven cottages in lower Broadway, beyond Hagbourne Road, known then as 'Newtown Terrace', erected 1885 (now nos 29–41 Broadway).

The West Curve and the Demolishment of Foxhall House

The Great Western Railway's west curve to the line was opened February 1886. It was constructed to provide a new link from Oxford and the north, to Swindon, and thence to Bristol in the west. Almost immediately, through services between Oxford and Weymouth were introduced. The west curve joined together the Oxford branch line and the London–Bristol main line in such a way that the station was bypassed, thus speeding up services.

To make way for the west curve and to create a site for the Provender Store, the early seventeenth-century Foxhall House and its farm buildings were demolished. The farm had been purchased by the GWR from Colonel Loyd-Lindsay in 1884; which had been bought by the latter from Jacob Appleford earlier in 1868. At the time of demolition, the house was tenanted by farm labourers.

The proper name for the farm should be Foxhall, and not Vauxhall. The latter spelling came from the vernacular pronunciation of the name: in the former Berkshire dialect an 'F' was always pronounced as 'V'; this is how Foxhall became Vauxhall.

A great myth has grown up around Foxhall House which is repeated over and over again: that the house was a hunting lodge for either James I or James II – those that tell the tale can never be certain as to which king was involved; apparently, these kings would hunt foxes there, hence the derivation of Foxhall.

Like all Didcot myths, this is arrant nonsense. Those who put forward the theory, and those who have repeated it over the years, never

A detail from the Stuart glass of James I or II which was formerly in old Foxhall House, demolished in 1884 by the GWR.

examined it in the cold light of day. Because if they had, they would realize it is just a fanciful story. It first appeared in the book, *The Upper Thames Valley*, by Lord Wyfold, in 1923; he states: '. . . Foxhall is traditionally said to have been a royal hunting box of the Monarch [James 1].' This item was taken from an extract which he found in the *Journal of the Berkshire Archaeological Society*. The story is based purely on the existence of a stained glass window that was once in Foxhall House. The window was/is composed of diamond shaped leaded glass, each pane containing the royal badge of James I, the rose of England and the thistle of Scotland. When the farmhouse was demolished, the glass was taken out, and made into a fire screen, which was placed in the GWR's boardroom at Paddington. During the last war, it suffered damage, was restored and then was presented to Reading Borough Council in 1946. It was on display in the town hall at Reading up to 1980. In 1981, the firescreen was in turn presented to the Didcot Town Council, where it can be seen today.

James I, like his predecessor, Elizabeth I, moved about the country with a vast retinue of courtiers, officials and servants, plus cart after cart loaded up with furniture, clothes, etc. Their needs could only be satisfied by a very large house, a mansion, and not a small four-bedroomed house such as that of Foxhall. It would have been no larger than Smiths Farm or 28–30 Manor Road.

Furthermore, had the king been visiting Didcot regularly, then some mention would have occurred in Didcot documents of the times, wills or parish registers. It is hardly conceivable that a king could come and go without a reference being made in some document, and there is none. Moreover, as a highly valuable item in the seventeenth century, the glass is not mentioned in any Didcot probate inventory. Had it been there in place, it would have been noted and valued.

Lastly, where did the glass come from? The Dandridge family, a well-known local family, who were quite prosperous, and lived at Foxhall from about 1716 to 1769, could have installed it. Though it is unlikely: the early eighteenth century was the time of the two Jacobite rebellions; to put in glass bearing the emblems of the Stuart kings would have been rather foolhardy. The likeliest candidate is Jacob Appleford. Mr Warner gave the clue in his article/obituary for Amy Strange, who knew Foxhall House before it was demolished in 1884. In the article, he wrote that at Foxhall lived Jacob Appleford, farmer and collector of antiques, which he used to adorn his house.

Before he sold Foxhall, he 'bought at a sale in Wantage, some oak panelling for the hall and stairway . . .'. Amy Strange also saw the glass in the windows of the hall. Is it not probable that Appleford bought the glass, and had it installed in the house and before 1868, the year in which he sold the house?

The Building of the Provender Store in 1884

The GWR acquired Foxhall House and its farm buildings in 1884, to create space for the Provender Store and then the west curve, constructed two years later, in 1886.

In 1906, the *Great Western Magazine* printed an article, entitled the 'Horse Provender Stores, Didcot', from which this description has been taken: The Provender Store was erected to provide provender or hay cut into chaff and corn which was crushed, the two mixed in equal parts that was then sent out as forage for the company's 3,000 horses, in use at the many stations throughout the Great Western Company's system.

Before 1884, the company's provender depot had been at Handsworth, but with the increase in the number of horses used, and

The Provender Store of 1884.

the need for more up-to-date methods, came the demand for larger premises in a more central position for efficient distribution. Didcot was chosen once again. Not only did Didcot occupy this central position, it was also in the middle of a large corn and hay growing area. The store provided both employment for about forty men and an outlet for farmers to sell their produce. By the end of the century, it was estimated that an area of approximately 9,000 acres was being utilized to grow hay, oats and beans for the Didcot store.

The dimensions of the main building, a brick-built structure, were about 202 ft long, 49 ft wide and 72 ft high, flanked on each side by a high tower carrying a large water tank. There were four floors. The upper floor was used for the storage of corn and for the chaff-cutting machinery, the next floor for hay sifters and corn mills, the floor below for the mixers, and the ground floor for receiving from the mixers the prepared forage to be placed into sacks and loaded on to wagons. Although space was provided on each floor for hay and straw storage before being processed, in time this proved insufficient so a large barn was erected behind the store in 1900, to give extra storage space for these reserves; the two were connected by a power elevator which delivered trusses of hay and straw to the top floor of the main building.

Originally, the Provender Store's machinery was driven by steam. In 1901, this was changed to electric power. The electrical power house was sited next to the hay barn, and contained two 100 horse power dynamos. Current was not only supplied to the store, but also to the pumping station at Appleford, and the power operated points and signals at Didcot. A hydraulic plant supplied power for the lifts and capstans, and two water pumps, one of which picked up water from the Thames at Appleford, sending it to the village reservoir which supplied both Didcot and Northbourne.

The contracts for the purchase of provender were made about every three months, and involved expenditure of roughly £70,000 per annum. Arrangements were made with the contractors for the supply of regular weekly quantities of the various kinds of provender. In 1906, the weekly requirements were 100 sacks of oats, 220 sacks of beans, 480 sacks of maize, 110 tons of hay, 16 tons of oat straw, 18 tons of bran and 40 or 50 tons of straw. The material had to be of the highest quality; and farmers soon learnt not to send in inferior material which would be rejected. The makeup of the feed and quantities were met by the GWR's Veterinary Department.

With the decline in the use of horses by the GWR during this

The house was built in 1898 for the Provender Store's manager. It stood at the entrance to the new car-park created when the Provender Store was demolished in the 1970s.

century, the value of the Provender Store also diminished, so much so that it was eventually closed in 1953. It still continued to be used by private firms until 1963; it was then closed permanently. The building was finally demolished in 1976.

There may have been another reason, possibly the major one, for the demolition of Foxhall House, and that was the wish to replace it with a modern house, built to house the Provender Store manager. This house formerly stood on the other side of Foxhall Railway Bridges, at the entrance to the car-park.

The Great Fire at Didcot Station in 1886

This highly destructive fire started Thursday 11 March 1886, at 1 p.m. It practically destroyed the station which had just been extensively redesigned and rebuilt. This rebuilding had taken place

The aftermath of the great fire at Didcot Station in 1886, showing the almost destroyed frontage.
(Laurie Didcock)

between 1882 and 1885. The earlier Brunel station with its overall roof was demolished, to make room for four instead of five platforms. The refashioned station incorporated a new stationmaster's house. This replaced the former house, which fronted 'The Barracks' at the top of Station Road. These alterations were demanded because of the vastly increased traffic that was arriving and departing daily. The newly constructed west curve, and the opening of the Didcot, Newbury and Southampton Railway, meant that services were coming from all the major points of the compass – from the north, south-east and west. Didcot was truly a major junction on the Great Western Railway's system.

The fire thus destroyed the newly rebuilt station: the down platform and the station entrance were especially damaged. *Jackson's Oxford Journal* reported the fire in its issue of 13 March:

> shortly before 1 o'clock on Thursday afternoon a fire broke out in one of the waiting rooms on the down platform of the GW station at Didcot Junction. The flames spread with such rapidity that in a very short time the refreshment rooms, offices etc. were ablaze as

Didcot Station, as remodelled after the fire, c. *1907.*

> well as the platform itself. The wind was blowing the flames towards the middle platform and with a view to preventing them crossing the station and catching the buildings on the up platform, the middle one was partially torn up by the railway men, and even as it was the up express passing the station at about quarter to two had difficulty in getting through. The Oxford Volunteer fire brigade were communicated with by telegraph and the steamer was promptly dispatched with several members of the brigade, and the immense quantity of water the engine was able to pour on the fire prevented it spreading, and was the means of saving a great deal of valuable property from destruction. The station which had been rebuilt had only very recently been finished, another will now have to be entirely built.

Before the Oxford brigade arrived, the blaze was being fought solely by the Harwell volunteer force; the two forces together brought the blaze under control. The fire over, the work of rebuilding began, so much so that at the end of 1886, the station was nearly rebuilt.

6

The Village of Didcot, 1880–1918

By 1880, the number of Didcot landowners had been reduced to six; all were now absentees, except the Rector; and they were Col. Loyd-Lindsay, the Revd J.K. Morrell, John Blagrave, the Revd Thomas Rennison, Queen's College, and the Rector. The most important of these were Col. Loyd-Lindsay, the Revd Morrell and John Blagrave. These three between them owned over 700 acres. In 1880 the parish acreage was 1,194 acres. Little is known about the last two landlords, other than those details given in Chapter 2. But Lieutenant-Colonel Loyd-Lindsay is a different case. A great deal is known about him.

Originally he was just Robert Lindsay, a son of General James Lindsay, and was closely related to the Earl of Crawford. In early life, Lindsay was a soldier and during the Crimean War won the VC for exceptional gallantry at the battles of Alma and Inkerman.

In 1858, he married Harriet, only child and heiress to Lord Overstone. After the marriage, he adopted his father-in-law's surname of Loyd, and became Colonel Loyd-Lindsay. As he and his wife shared Lord Overstone's interest in agriculture, estate management and politics, Loyd-Lindsay retired from the army with the rank of lieutenant-colonel. The young couple then moved to Lockinge House, Lockinge – the house and manor of East Lockinge were given to them by Lord Overstone.

It was after the move to Lockinge that the Loyd-Lindsays, with the help of Lord Overstone, began to build up the vast Loyd estate in North Berkshire. This process had actually started back in the early 1850s: Manor Farm, Didcot, was an early acquisition, purchased 1857. In 1873, a survey which at the time was called a second

Lord Wantage, 1832–1901.

Domesday, found that Col. Loyd-Lindsay owned the largest acreage, some 20,000 acres, in Berkshire; an estate that was larger than that owned by the Earl of Craven.

The Loyd estate at Didcot was made up of Manor, Foxhall, Ladygrove and Bests Farms, plus a number of houses and cottages in the village, all purchased between 1858 and 1869. By 1880, this Didcot estate had been reorganized, and now consisted of just two farms – Manor and Ladygrove Farms. He also owned a considerable amount of land in East Hagbourne and Blewbury. He was also Lord of the Manor of Didcot and East Hagbourne.

Col. Loyd-Lindsay was a man of great influence in the two villages. Described as a tall, handsome, fair-haired man of athletic build, he was very much the aristocrat, as well as a friend of royalty, especially the Prince of Wales – who came to Didcot Station twice when visiting Lockinge, and was warmly greeted by locals. He could be autocratic when thwarted – witness the row with Robert Rich over the Northbourne board school in 1891 – but was generally kind and benevolent. Both he and his wife, as did Lord Overstone, shared enlightened ideas, which were distinctive considering his rank and the times. The model cottages at Lockinge are a good example of his concern for his farmworkers.

Col. Loyd-Lindsay was also interested in politics and became MP for Berkshire. Forced to retire from parliament twenty years later, he was offered a peerage and became Baron Wantage of Lockinge. He died in 1901, his estate passing to Lady Wantage – they were childless. She died in 1921.

The two farms, or Manor and Ladygrove Farms, owned by Lord Wantage at Didcot during this period were held by just five tenants. Manor Farm, in Foxhall Road, in 1880, was still tenanted by Benjamin Leach. He held the lease until about 1884. The next to hold the tenancy was George Napper, of Lime Tree Farm, East Hagbourne. He had been farming at Didcot since the mid-1870s, as tenant of Morrells Farm, though not resident at Didcot. In 1881, he and his family were still living at Lime Tree Farm, though it's not clear whether or not Napper and his family moved to Didcot after acquiring the lease to Manor Farm or stayed at East Hagbourne. Possibly they did. However, by 1887, George Napper had died, leaving his widow, Mrs George (or Mary) Napper as tenant of the two farms, with a combined acreage of 400 acres. She continued to hold the tenancies until about 1890, when her second son, Dennis Napper, took over the farms. It may be that this happened after his marriage, in about 1891.

During this period prior to the First World War, Dennis Napper's position in the life and affairs of the parish was almost paramount, though secondary to that of the parson, the Revd John Brown, the Rector, the undoubted leader of the parish. But Dennis Napper was always regarded as the 'Squire' of Didcot. To his workers he was 'The Boss'. In 1899, he bought Morrells Farm; though it was more commonly known as 'Hobbs Farm', after the then occupants, an aged couple named Hobbs, who just rented the house from Dennis Napper. After the tenancy had passed to the Nappers in the 1870s, Morrells Farm lost its independent status. Afterwards, the farmhouse continued to be tenanted mainly by farm labourers.

Both farmhouses were sited in Foxhall Road, quite close to each other. Manor Farmhouse still exists, and is now sheltered housing for older residents. Morrells Farmhouse, which formerly lay opposite Smiths Farm, was sited on the north corner of Manor Road. It was demolished in the 1950s, as were its farm buildings. The largest barn

Dennis Napper and his family in about 1908. *(John Lay)*

is now the Conservative Club. This former barn is the last of the six large barns that once existed in Didcot.

The 400 acres Dennis Napper farmed made him the most important farmer in Didcot, and helped to establish his future fortune. He was a dealer as well as farmer, and held one of the contracts to supply the Provender Store with fodder. This contract was one of the means by which Dennis Napper became rich. He was a shrewd, able man, and a fine businessman. He was no fool, and could be an autocrat with his men. But on the other hand, he was a kind and considerate employer, who would look after them at times of trouble – if ill or hurt in an accident. He employed about twenty men from the village as labourers, and women as servants.

He continued to increase his wealth. In 1921, he bought from Lady Wantage, Manor and Ladygrove Farms. At the time of his death in 1942, his estate consisted of these farms: Challow Marsh Farm; Little Circourt Farm, Denchworth; Grove Manor Farm; Morrells Farm and Manor Farm, Didcot; Brook Furlong Farm, East Hagbourne; Hunts Grave's Farm, Blewbury; with land in Brightwell;

Morrells Farm as seen from the meadows that then existed in the centre of the village.

Manor Road before the First World War. The house (now nos 28–30) just beyond White Cottage was the home for some forty years of William Napper. It was then known as Ladygrove Farm. *(C.J. Milne)*

land and two cottages at East Hagbourne; School House and the shop at Didcot; plus these cottages in Didcot: Marsh Cottages, two in Lydalls Lane, two cottages near the blacksmith's shop in Manor Road, two opposite the Queen's Arms; and three cottages (one house), in lower Manor Road.

Lord Wantage's other tenant was William Napper; he was probably George Napper's nephew. His father, also William, came to Didcot in about 1869, and took over one of George Napper's tenancies at Didcot, the lease to a small parcel of land, some 8 acres, from Thame School. William, Snr, also came to Didcot as Lord Wantage's tenant to Bests Farm, after the Buckles had given up the lease.

William Napper, Jnr, had by 1881 taken over these leases, and was then living at Bests Farmhouse (28–30 Manor Road), in Manor Road. When the lease to Ladygrove Farm became available in the 1880s, it was acquired by Napper, and added to Bests Farm, thus creating the new farm, Ladygrove, consisting of 143 acres. Ladygrove Farmhouse was thus another of those houses, which after losing its former status, was reduced to cottages for farm labourers, and usually occupied by two families. At one time, it was abandoned, and was taken over by gypsies. It was through this amalgamation that the name 'Ladygrove' was transferred to Napper's house in Manor Road.

Manor Road as would have been seen by Walter Davies when he was a boy during the Edwardian period. The village shop can be seen, then part of Manor Cottage. *(Don Farnborough)*

This is how the confusion over the precise location of Ladygrove Farm came about.

Though the farmhouse in Manor Road still exists, its farm buildings were demolished after the last war. The large barn was burnt down during the war: it is said that a courting couple caused the fire, by dropping a cigarette. The owner had a heart attack and died on hearing the news.

William Napper also built the terrace of six cottages in Lydalls Road (nos 127–37), formerly known as 'Church View' – a commemorative tablet with 'W.N. 1893' is fixed to the front elevation.

So during the late nineteenth century the Napper clan reigned supreme throughout the three villages, Didcot and East and West Hagbourne: they rented or owned many of the farms, and also controlled all the public houses in the Hagbournes.

As the landowners had been reduced in number after 1880, so had the number of farms: basically there were five, and at times four. The fifth farm was the Glebe; sometimes this had a separate existence, sometimes not. In 1880, it was a separate unit, when rented out to Thomas Freeguard of Blenheim House. Later it was held by William

Church View, 127–37 Lydalls Roads, which were erected by William Napper in 1893. *(Don Farnborough)*

Napper, and added to Ladygrove Farm. The lease was acquired by Napper from the Rector in the 1890s.

The other two farms were Blagraves Farm and Smiths Farm. In 1880, James Turner was still tenant of Blagraves Farm, which had been reduced from its former acreage of 203 to 167 acres. By 1890, the lease had passed to a George Perry; as he was there until at least the First World War, the farm became known as 'Perry's Farm'. As mentioned previously, in 1899 this farm was acquired by Robert Rich. George Perry was also the licencee of The Royal Oak, at Station Approach, which he also rented from John Blagrave. This house has now been demolished.

The two other Didcot farms had also been incorporated into one, and were those owned by the Revd Rennison, Bursar of Queen's College (this was the former Taylor Farm), and Queen's College. They had been a single unit, with the Rector's Glebe, for nearly a century, and had been held as such by the Taylors during that time. When William Taylor died and his farm sold to Rennison, the former at the time of his death was still renting the Glebe. Rennison's new tenant, Henry Smith, held the three for a short while, but soon lost the Glebe to Thomas Freeguard.

Henry Smith on his move to Didcot, moved into 'Taylors Farm', and through the family's long association with this farm, the house has become known as 'Smiths Farm', and is still known thus today, even though the Smiths sold the farm to the Rymans in 1935. The farmhouse and some of the farm buildings stand on the corner of Brasenose Road.

At the turn of the century, Henry Smith had quite an infamous reputation in the village, and was known as 'Bodger' Smith. He lived with his unmarried sons and daughters – the youngest, Sidney, was a butcher in West Street, Northbourne – at Smiths Farm; and they all shared a common failing, a love of strong drink. They spent more time propping up the bar of the Old Wheatsheaf Inn in the Wantage Road than they did farming. Henry was known as 'Bodger', because he was exactly that. The farm buildings were in a ruinous state and his fields choked with weeds, which made hard work for their men.

There were many other small pieces of land, the 8 acres mentioned earlier, owned by Thame School, was one. None was larger than 10 acres, and had different owners. Each of the hotels at the station had its accompanying field for the grazing of horses, either belonging to the hotel or to guests.

There was one smallholding known as Davis' Farm, of nearly

3 acres. It was rented by George Davis from Lord Wantage. His farm, of which the larger part lay in East Hagbourne, was on the south side of what is now the Broadway. The farmhouse, or 'New House' as it was known, formerly stood at the corner of Foxhall Road–Broadway; and was known locally as Davis' Corner.

Didcot village at this time was an enclosed world, its horizons limited to parochial affairs, where news of the outside world, sometimes long after the event, came via the village pub or shop. As has been shown, life was hard, diseases, especially diphtheria and scarlet fever, were always present. Conditions were primitive. Houses were damp and draughty, no hot and cold running water, coal fires, paraffin lamps for candles for lighting, and earth closets in the back gardens. Wages for farm workers at this time ranged from 15*s.* (75p), to about £1.

Life may have been hard for the villagers but in the main they were reasonably happy with their lot. It was a tightly knit community, where everybody knew each other, and were looked after during times of trouble. Crime and violence hardly ever occurred and when they did came from outsiders. Conditions were primitive, but it was what they were used to and expected.

Prior to 1914, Didcot village was virtually the same as it had been for centuries before. Though during the period 1840–75, many of the earlier timber-framed houses and cottages went, such as the Queen's College House or the early Rectory, many survived. The village in this period did have great charm as postcards of the period show: its period houses and Victorian cottages set out around its ancient streets and village greens, the meadows with numerous trees, great elms and oaks, hedges and, in summer, a profusion of wild flowers.

Manor Road was either known as Down Street or High Street, and around by the Queen's Arms, as Queen's Street. Britwell Road was also known as 'Long Strings Lane' after the Long Strings Furlong that ran down by the road. Lydalls Lane or Road is early eighteenth century in date, and is derived from the Lydalls family. Downs Road is medieval.

One reason for the relative happiness of the villagers was that the majority of them all belonged to the same class – the working class – so there were no great social divisions between them. The middle class was represented by the relatively few farmers and, in particular, the parson or the Rector, John Brown, and Arthur Stevens at Britwell Lodge.

The Rector was the Revd John Brown, MA, Rector of All Saints (1890–1922), who was the undoubted leader of that rural community prior to the Great War. This position was derived from his social class, education, income and office. His influence was considerable. He, a tall, stout man, received a large income from the parish, so was able to enjoy a comfortable lifestyle at the Rectory, where he employed villagers, women as house servants and about six or more men as gardeners.

His attitudes to religion were strong and uncompromising. He was actively involved in local politics as Chairman of the parish council from 1894 to 1919, and the Didcot member of the Wallingford Rural District Council, and its Chairman 1907–12. So it's small wonder that the village women would curtsey and men touch their caps as he passed by. Though he and Dennis Napper were the village leaders, the Rector would always come first, because he was a gentleman; the latter wasn't.

The other man of standing in the parish, and who was also a gentleman, was Arthur Stevens, of Britwell Lodge. Strictly speaking, he was not a member of the community in that he did not live in the village, where his influence was slight, but he was respected by the villagers. A man of independent means, he lived with his two unmarried daughters, the two Misses Stevens. He too employed women servants and men as gardeners, all from the village. William Lewthwaite was at one time his head gardener. Arthur Stevens died April 1914.

He was also responsible, in 1897, for making Britwell Road a private carriage road which had become by common usage a public right of way, stopping the road at the Broadway end by posts and bar. They were still there in the 1940s.

There were others who also had their place in the community, and were important in their different ways: they were the schoolteacher, and the two shopkeepers.

The schoolmistress before the First World War was Miss Skyrmer who came to Didcot in the early 1880s. Initially she taught with an assistant in the old schoolroom. This was built in 1854 and was located at the rear of the Rectory Cottages in Lydalls Road.

Didcot's first school opened in 1847. Before the building of the schoolroom school may have been held in the vestry. There was a succession of school teachers until the arrival of Miss Skyrmer. In 1896 the schoolroom was replaced by a new school – the Board or Elementary School in Manor Road (now Manor Road Infants).

The Board School in the old village, opened in 1894. *(Don Farnborough)*

There was no controversy over the establishment of this Board School, simply because the old order, in the form of the Rector, controlled it – and control it he did. He came every week to give religious lessons.

Miss Skyrmer became its first headmistress, with a staff of four. The school was built on what was formerly the site of the Queens College farmhouse. The farmhouse had been burnt down previously, but its associated farm buildings and the large barn were demolished to make way for the school. The school building was enlarged in 1903 to take 185 children, and again in 1910. Despite its capacity, on average only 105 children attended.

There had been a shop in Didcot Village since before 1734 in Manor Road. It was located in what is now known as Manor Cottage which is next to the school. In the 1880s the shopkeeper was Miss Ann Appleford, a daughter of Jacob Appleford. In 1895 she was described as a grocer and provision dealer. In 1899 the shop was bought by Mrs Patience Napper of Harwell. By 1910 a Mr and Mrs Robbins ran the shop, and were still there in the 1920s. The shop was then bought by Dennis Napper in 1919.

Mrs Robbins sold everything the village women might need. Generally they paid their bills weekly – 'on the slate' – but they had to catch their husbands before they got to the pub on paydays. The village shop was handy for the village women. If a wider choice was needed they had to go to Northbourne, which tended to be an expedition as it was over a mile away. But there were more shops: a baker, butcher and other grocery shops plus a haberdashery shop. A travelling baker also came from Upton.

The other shop during this period was sited in the first house in Manor Road (no. 49). It was known by the name of its occupant, or 'Jennie Fullers'. This was a typical parlour shop, from which the owner sold sweets and other confectionery. The parlour windows were filled with sweet jars, an instant attraction to the village children who would spend their pennies in her shop.

The working class villagers made up the remainder of that pre-1914 population of Old Didcot. They worked as farm labourers, gardeners or as house servants. Some of the families living there still have descendants in Didcot today. The Woodleys and Talbots, for instance, have lived in the parish since 1770 and 1807 respectively. John, William and George Woodley were the village blacksmiths from 1776 until the late nineteenth century. The Blissets became the village blacksmiths after the Woodleys gave up the shop.

The village still had its foreign element in the railwaymen; a small enclave was living in old Didcot, despite the existence of Northbourne, and its houses easily available for rent. They formed a tightly knit group, living close together in the newly built cottages – 'Church View'. These were built specifically for the railwaymen to rent. The villagers called this part of Lydalls Lane the 'posh end'. The two groups never did mix. Their backgrounds, economic circumstances and jobs were so dissimilar that their only common ground – if that – was the village pub.

7

Didcot at the Turn of the Century, 1899–1912

At the turn of this century, Old Didcot and Northbourne were still set in a rural landscape, even though the seeds of their future expansion had already been sown – not that anyone living at that time was aware of that fact – and were remote, isolated from any urban centre, especially London. Robert Rich's purchase of Blagraves Farm in 1899 almost guaranteed that Didcot would grow, though years might pass before this growth would become apparent.

In the year 1900, the old village and Newtown were still distinct communities with well-defined boundaries. There was no ribbon development to link them indecisively. The wide expanse of farmland that lay between the two communities created the physical division; the animosity that existed between their inhabitants created the other, the mental division.

Before the Great War, the area of the civil parish of Didcot was half of what it is today: its southern boundary the Broadway–Wantage Road. The northern edge of this road was then the boundary between Didcot and East and West Hagbourne. In 1935, boundaries were extended southward to take in a major part of these parishes.

The Broadway–Wantage Road (an ancient roadway, almost certainly pre-Roman), was then a narrow country lane, which meandered through the countryside, with field and meadow on either side and bordered by large elm trees. Before 1914, only three houses were sited alongside the road, west of Northbourne, and of these two were inns, the old White Hart and the old Wheatsheaf, and the other a farmhouse, Davis' Farm or New House.

The Wantage Road (now Broadway) in c. *1910, showing the houses built between 1905 and 1912. The semi-detached house on the immediate right was demolished to make way for the former Woolworth Stores.*
(Don Farnborough)

To the north-east of the village was the railway station with its three houses and shop set out around a large roundabout known locally as Station Approach. The station was connected to the Wallingford Road by Station Road or 'Station Hill', as it was known before the last war.

Farmland was the dominant feature of that landscape, so much so that if it were possible to go back in time and stand in the Broadway facing west all that could be seen would be open space. A panoramic view would take in the embankment of the Didcot–Newbury–Southampton Railway and St Andrew's Church tower, with East Hagbourne village, obscured by its trees, in the south. The Broadway was a narrow tree-lined lane disappearing into the west. The village of Didcot lay on its ridge, also obscured by trees and separated from the road by farmland, with the station at the bottom of the slope to the north. The little hills and slopes that are such a feature of Didcot's landscape would be easily seen. Lastly, to the east would be Didcot New Town or Northbourne.

Trees were everywhere – except in Northbourne. In fact they were as much a feature of the landscape as was farmland. As mentioned

Britwell Road in 1940, then a quiet rural lane; this is just one view of the appearance of Didcot at the turn of the century.

above, the Broadway was tree lined, especially on the south side. Tradition has it that the elms sited along the road were planted by Lady Wantage during the second half of the century – and it may well be true.

All the ancient roads in the district, before 1900 – Old Didcot village streets, Foxhall Road, Park Road, Wantage Road, Broadway, Abingdon Road and Cow Lane – were extremely narrow country lanes, varying from 12 to 16½ ft in width (a legacy from earlier centuries when wide roads were not required), and pre-date the sixteenth century. The Broadway–Wantage Road is probably pre-Roman.

Many reports were made in the 1890s and 1900s to the Wallingford Rural District Council about the condition of these roads. In 1895 and 1901, the County Surveyor reported that 'the roads throughout the district were in a bad state', and, in particular, it was reported that,

> in Park Lane two vehicles could hardly pass each other and the sides shelve off so rapidly in places that a loaded wagon making

Park Lane in the 1920s. The boy, George Hughes, a member of the Moxon family, stands where, some years later, the entrance to the canning factory would be.

(David Moxon)

> room for another could easily lose a portion of its load [and for] a cyclist could be extremely dangerous. Park Lane was much used by heavy traffic conveying straw and other goods to the goods station at Didcot.

As the main road from the village to the station, Lydalls Lane was particularly narrow. At that time it was the only way to get to the station, other than using Station Road. Lower Lydalls Road was then named Hadden Lane. In 1907, it was widened to 36 ft, and the acute bend just beyond the junction of Manor Road–Lydalls Road was straightened. It was also resurfaced.

The stretch of Manor Road from White Cottage to the Queen's Arms and its junction with Lydalls Road was little more than a footpath, and barred by three posts at Hitchman's Corner (by White Cottage; named after its then occupant). The posts were removed and the road widened to its present width. The roads had to be widened in response to increasing traffic going to the station.

Every road had its accompanying drainage ditches, one on each side, which were usually choked up with vegetation, rubbish and sewage, causing widespread flooding, often for weeks at a time during winter. It was especially bad at the station, lying as it does at the bottom of a slope. Other troublesome spots were the Marsh Railway Bridge and the ford at East Hagbourne. The council in those days waged a continual battle to get the ditches – they were all on private land – cleaned, but with indifferent results; and flooding occurred every year.

In 1907, a Mary James of 9 Hadden Lane complained to the council 'that the ditch there was a disgrace [and] that she and a young friend fell into an open ditch opposite her home and ruined their dresses'. One does wonder how she managed to fall into an open ditch which must have been quite deep and was probably full of sewage.

Another problem was the motor car which first appeared on Didcot's streets in the early 1900s. Because of its relative higher speeds to that of the slower horse-drawn wagons and carriages, the motor car tended to damage delicate road surfaces, with resulting high repair costs to the ratepayer. The early heavy motor lorries which began to appear in greater numbers were especially disliked. The damage they did was considerable. The council in 1903 and 1907 tried to impose speed limits of 10 miles or less, especially through villages, but without success. Later speed limits were dropped in favour of warning motorists about dangerous driving. Motor traffic in those early days was always a nuisance, but the motor car was here to stay.

During that final decade before the outbreak of war, building operations moved away from Northbourne, to the area between it and the station. Emphasis was at first on ribbon development, as house building spread along the Wallingford Road, Station Road and Hadden Lane (now lower Lydalls Road).

Also during that decade two large and prominent buildings were erected in the Wallingford Road, sited next door to each other: the Methodist Church and the former St Peter's Vicarage. They stood opposite the present main post office. The vicarage was demolished in 1986, to be replaced by Didcot's latest building, the Baptist House. At the beginning of the early 1950s, the former was sold by the Church Commissioners to the Wallingford Rural District Council, to

St Peter's Vicarage, built in 1908 and shown here in the early 1970s when it was part of the Wallingford RDC's offices.

be used as their offices. The authority in turn sold the building and site for redevelopment in 1985. The Wesleyans (now Methodists) built their church in 1903, on land sold to them by Lady Wantage. She also had the vicarage built, in 1908, and gave the land on which it stood. The first curate to live in the house was the Revd F. Urch. He was followed by Lady Wantage's nephew, the Hon. and Revd E.R. Lindsay. He took up residence in the new vicarage, with a domestic staff including a butler. How did *he* get on with the railwaymen, when there were no points of contact? Was he another parson like his superior, the Revd Baker of East Hagbourne? Lady Wantage built the vicarage so that the clergy would have a suitable place in which to live. She did not think rooms in a house in East Street quite suitable. She was a deeply religious woman so it does seem fitting that the vicarage has been replaced by a building that houses another religious organization.

The other large building to have been erected during this time was the former police station in Hagbourne Road, in 1912.

It was Robert Rich who started the next phase in the expansion of Didcot, when he erected a terrace of six cottages in Hadden Lane, in

South Street or Wessex Road and Didcot's first police station of 1912. This detail comes from a post-card of c. 1919.

1901. These were the first of the many houses to be built between Northbourne and Old Didcot, after 1900.

The next houses to be erected, a more ambitious programme, were the GWR cottages in Station Road, in 1903. There were thirty-two, and were occupied according to rank within the railway hierarchy; the lowest were housed farther up the hill, the more senior nearer the station. The stationmaster was given a new, large detached house near to the station which replaced the one within the station itself.

The stationmaster's former house at the top of Station Road became Didcot's post office from 1878 until 1939. It was replaced by the present building in the latter year. Before 1878, the post office had been housed in one of a set of two cottages at the station, near the Cow Lane railway bridge. It had been established there in 1860.

Station Road was opened in 1847. It was laid out on land acquired from Revd W.R. Baker. The land took the form of a strip which ran up from the station to the Wallingford Road. The road having been laid down, the remainder of the strip was left unused; in the late nineteenth century, it was used as allotments, until it was needed for the GWR cottages. It is odd that the GWR took so long to build

Station Hill during the first years of this century. The GWR houses of 1904 had just been built. The post office was then established in the large house at the top of the hill. Originally the house had been built in 1852, as the stationmaster's residence. This is where Mr Peach lived in 1861.
(Don Farnborough)

houses for their workers, considering the need back much earlier in the 1840s and '50s and not at the time they were built, when there were plenty of houses available for renting.

The GWR had continued the movement to build in the centre. It was soon followed by other developers who, having acquired building land from Robert Rich, started to erect houses along the Wallingford Road or Hadden Lane during the years 1905 to 1911.

The key to this new development was the acquisition by Robert Rich and Dennis Napper of Blagraves Farm and Morrells Farm, in 1899 and 1903 respectively. With control of a major part of Didcot's farmland, and in such a strategic position, passing from their former wealthy owners to these two local men, both of whom saw nothing wrong in selling land for speculative building, the way was now clear for the long term expansion of Didcot.

Rich's purchase, Blagraves Farm, in particular, had one large field near the station, of 40 acres, bounded by Britwell Road, Wallingford Road, Hadden Lane and by the boundary created by the back

Haymaking in Ryman's Meadow (now the site of Blenheim Close) immediately adjacent to Britwell Lodge, which was then the home of the Ryman family.

gardens of the Station Road houses. This was the most valuable piece of land in the future expansion of Didcot. It included the Wallingford Road frontage on which the Broadway shopping centre now stands.

Both Rich and Napper were only too aware of the wealth to be had in house building on a large scale and for rent. Consequently, both, one after another, produced ambitious housing estate plans. Though they were not the first: the Newbury Land and Building Company had equally ambitious plans in 1882, which ended in bankruptcy.

Dennis Napper was next to produce an estate plan, in 1903. The plan was for twelve villas to be built along the Harwell Road (upper Broadway), and seventy-four cottages on either side of a new road that was to run parallel with the latter road, from the old White Hart in Station Road to New House or Davis' Farm at the bottom of Foxhall Road.

As in the case of the earlier company, Napper's plan also came to nothing – though it did get as far as the local authority conducting a survey of levels for installation of sewage and water connections to the proposed houses. His plan was odd in more than one way. For instance, why this very long road when six or more shorter

The Wallingford Road at about the time of the First World War.

north–south roads would have been more sensible? Possibly, he was constrained by the layout of the site on which the estate was to be built. Unfortunately, as the plan no longer exists (as far as we know), we will never know precisely the shape of his design. The other curious fact concerns the land itself, which Napper did not own. The owners were Lady Wantage and Robert Rich. Presumably Napper had secured an option which lapsed when the scheme was abandoned.

But he did build one of the villas. This was known as 'Sunnyside' and stood roughly where the W.H. Smith's shop is now sited. It was demolished about 1960. In later years it was occupied by Trents, the dentists.

Napper was followed by Rich who, in 1905, produced his own scheme. This was for an estate of 441 houses to be built in the field near the station, mentioned earlier, and was to be known as the Junction Estate. It was bounded by the Wallingford Road and Hadden Lane which were to be the frontages of the new estate. There were to be three new roads, with houses built on each side. A fourth road was also planned, to which houses, presumably, would be added at a later date.

It was an enormous estate for Didcot at that time; and you might wonder where on earth the tenants were to come from. Rich was hardly the best of builders – nor the best landlord. He was one, it seems, who could be indifferent to the pleas of tenants. We can be thankful it was never built.

This scheme and others like it were welcomed by the Rural District Council. Members saw quite clearly the value of such estates in that they increased considerably the rateable value of the area. The heavy costs of the sewage and water supply schemes then being introduced into Northbourne and Old Didcot fell on to the ratepayers of the whole district, who obviously wanted the load eased.

Once again, this scheme also failed. But it still stayed in his mind. Rich was tinkering with modifications to the plan as late as 1914. S. Allen Warner, who knew Rich, wrote that

> this plan of Mr. Rich was subsequently much modified and instead of three roads north and south, a wide road from the 'White Hart' to the station was proposed, with an open square and a sort of market place with shops on three sides was to have been built where the present-day shops and offices now stand – so many have been the changes of plans during the course of years. The 1914–18 war brought all building schemes to an end.

Although Robert Rich's housing estate scheme may have come to naught, he did get as far as laying out the 'wide road' as mentioned by S. Allan Warner. The course of the road was laid down in 1910: its line is shown quite clearly in the large-scale Ordnance Survey Map of 1933. Presumably it was one of the two roads that Rich had informed the Rural District Council he would be laying down that year. The road ran from behind the Prince of Wales, across Hadden Lane and ended at the west side of the junction of Station Road and the Wallingford Road. A piece of the garden of 63 Lydalls Road was sliced off to allow the road to travel in a straight line from Hadden Lane up to the Wallingford Road. An alley running around to the back of nos 45–63 is presumably its last remnant.

Rich was a man of many parts, with more than one scheme being developed. One of these was his sidings – now known as Rich's Sidings. Of course today it is no longer a siding as it was originally, now it's a small business estate. But back at the turn of the century when it was being developed, it was just that – a long siding – one which nearly reached the road, with a number of spurs. Rich acted as agent on behalf of a number of small tradesmen who contracted with him for the trans-shipment of goods to his sidings. Though coal was the main shipment, to George Warwick, coal merchant of East Hagbourne, it was easier for Warwick to collect it from Rich's sidings, than go to the goods shed at the back of the station via Foxhall Road and the railway bridges. Rich rented the sidings from the GWR and paid a charge for every wagon that was shunted to the Sidings.

Though Rich never proceeded with the housing estate, he did build a few houses along the Harwell Road (upper Broadway) and Hadden Lane. He had started with the six cottages in Hadden Lane (or Lydalls Road) of 1901. These preceded the estate plan, by some four years. They were nos 45–55; and he probably built the pair immediately adjacent, nos 57–63. On earlier maps, these cottages can be seen as an integral group. Another set of cottages built by him is in the Abingdon Road, opposite and just south of the former exit to Cow Lane. Rich lived in one during the first years of the century until he moved to 'Richmead', which he built in 1919.

He sold more sites in Hadden Lane, and on these, subsequently, nos 9–39 were erected in 1907 to 1909, by a Mr Corderoy. These, too, should be seen as a single group. He very probably was also responsible for another terrace, of four houses, farther up, in Lydalls Road, opposite Blagraves Farm, at about the same time.

Several houses were erected in Harwell Road by Rich and one or

Houses in Lydalls Road (nos 109–15), erected c. *1908.*

two other jobbing builders, on sites sold by him. Rich built at least two of the houses. One house, now unoccupied and boarded up, which stands next to the fire station, was built by George Hobbs in 1907. By 1914, seven houses had been put up – four sets of semis and three that were detached.

The final feature of the decade was the building of new shops: the two in lower Lydalls Road of 1910, and the two Bosleys' shops in Wallingford Road of 1907, one of which sold bicycles. The blacksmith's shop next door had been established at the end of the previous century.

The last building to be erected before the outbreak of war was the old police station, and that in 1912.

An era had ended; 1914 and the Great War heralded a new age.

8

The Great War and Didcot, 1914–1915

The Great War began on 4 August 1914. To most people the outbreak of war did not come as a surprise: Germany had been recognized as the potential enemy for many years. Mr Hector Cullen of Newlands Avenue, who was 14 in 1914, well remembers as a child in 1908 reading a weekly magazine which had as its serial a story of war with Germany.

The war was greeted with great patriotic fervour. The country accepted that the war had come as long prophesied, and the nation would have to take on the Hun, and thrash him as quickly as possible. Looking back now, we know only too well how naïve that generation was, which found to their terrible cost just how horrific modern war could be. But this attitude was changed as the demands on the country grew ever greater, for more and more men, supplies and munitions. Not only was there this patriotic fervour, there was also tension and fear among the general population. The railways – the tracks or the 'metals', bridges and culverts – were guarded constantly against saboteurs. In that pre-motor age, the railways were vital to the war effort. As in the last war, the population was on its guard against fifth columnists. In August 1914, the police had been told to keep an eye on strangers. Consequently, any stranger was viewed with great suspicion. At Uffington, in August, a photographer with an hour to kill started to sketch the White Horse Hill. Within minutes he was surrounded by a crowd of villagers and accused of being a 'German spy'. He, a Mr Adams, had great difficulty persuading the local policeman that he was innocent. Finally, he had to produce his passport to prove his identity.

The country began to mobilize quickly. On 8 August at Wallingford, a crowd gathered outside the main post office expecting an urgent order for the territorials to get ready to march. It came and the local company marched to the railway station on their way to the territorial HQ at Reading. They were cheered off by a large crowd. All over the country territorial reserves were being mobilized. In September, an advert appeared telling the 4th (Reserve Battalion), Royal Berkshire Regiment (ages 19–35), to muster as Reading for general service. At Wallingford, also in September, recruiting was in full swing: every town sending its full quota. The *Berks and Oxon Advertizer* proudly reported that some small villages were sending as many as eight or ten young men. Wallingford and surrounding villages, including Old Didcot and Northbourne, sent many men. In July 1915, the paper reported 'about 90 officers and men belonging to the Berkshire Regiment visited Didcot for the purpose of getting new recruits. Parading through the village and then to Harwell, a recruiting meeting was held in the evening opposite the White Hart.'

Churn, above Blewbury, acted as a holding camp for the men of these yeomanry regiments. Churn and this part of the Downs had been a centre for army manoeuvres from 1889 onwards. During late 1914, many thousands were encamped there; and reported as being 'well behaved'. The army commandeered use of the Didcot, Newbury and Southampton Railway; and on 1 August, the line was given up entirely to the transport of troops. This seems to have been the case throughout August.

This part of North Berkshire was also given over to troop training. On 30 October, it was reported that manoeuvres were taking place in the open fields and on Wittenham Clumps, and 'on Tuesday, a midnight attack was made on the town [Wallingford]. There was sound of gunfire, and that of horses galloping through the street in the early hours – but the citizens had been informed.' By the end of October, all troops had left Churn.

The war was soon to affect Didcot, in fact, even before its outbreak. The government was only too aware of the vulnerability of the railway system that was vital to the war effort, for the movement of men and supplies, especially munitions. Sabotage of the lines in a war situation was an ever present possibility and the army took such threats seriously. The railways had been guarded before in 1911, at the time of the Agadir Crisis – when Germany sent a gunboat to this Moroccan port; it seemed then that the country was on the verge of war. Thus in August 1914, the railways were quickly put under guard. Mr Cullen remembers only too clearly two platelayers guarding the Foxhall railway bridges – and this was before the outbreak of hostilities.

Mr Cullen was well placed, even as a young boy of 14 years, to observe the activities of the military at Didcot. He was then living in the house that was (and still is) sited between the two bridges, known as Foxhall. His father, Mr W.E. Cullen, was the manager of the Provender Store, having been appointed in October 1913.

He was another of those prominent men of the earlier years of this century, and will be well remembered by older residents. Mr Cullen, Snr, was an astute businessman, and like Robert Rich was very enterprising. He built the two cinemas, in 1926 and 1933 respectively. The earlier cinema was demolished recently to make way for the new library. He also built one of the two shops which formed part of the former International Stores, and erected the first of the many houses that would stand between the old Wheatsheaf Inn and the former St Peter's Vicarage in the Broadway. This was the bungalow, at 195 Broadway, in 1919. Like all good businessmen, he kept his eyes open, and clearly saw the opportunities that existed, especially in those early postwar years. These business ventures were put in motion when he was still manager of the Provender Store, and an employee of the Great Western Company.

The platelayers were replaced by soldiers who came to Didcot in early August. They were men from the 1st Battalion, the 5th 'King's Own', the Royal Lancaster Regiment. The battalion had arrived by train from Lancaster on 14 August; their orders were to guard a section of the railway from Reading to Swindon. Brigadier-General Hibbert and his staff had travelled down on the same train, which arrived at Didcot about 9 p.m. No billets had been arranged and it was decided to bivouac for the night. Brigade and battalion headquarters as well as transport stores, were set up at Didcot, and after a conference orders were issued. The seven companies of the battalion were to be entrained by 9 a.m. on the 15th, each company taking over a stretch of the line. Men were stationed along the line at intervals, with a post at each bridge and station. Mr Cullen also remembers that the Foxhall railway bridges were guarded by a Sergeant Haig, and three men. His mother used to cook their Sunday lunch; their quarters, a hut at the bridge.

Culverts were also watched. Four companies moved west towards Swindon and three east towards Reading, with 'D' company guarding the Didcot stretch. Later in August, the *Berks and Oxon*

An infantry group at Churn during the First World War.

Advertizer reported that the bridges were watched during the day by boy scouts; and at night, presumably, by soldiers.

Sabotage was obviously a constant threat; especially after the battalion actually did catch two men on the railway, who were found to be carrying dynamite caps in their pockets. The accommodation at many of the bridges was bad; and the men were living under active service conditions little better than they later experienced in France. In addition patrolling the line was often dangerous, and casualties, sometimes fatal, occurred at times. Their presence was equally dangerous to civilians, for more than one man who would or did not stop when challenged was actually shot and wounded. At Taplow Bridge, in September, a man who was shot in this way subsequently died of his wounds. Later it was discovered that he was mentally disturbed. Early in September 1914, a draft of 200 men arrived from Lancaster, where they had just been recruited. Their arrival brought battalion strength up to 1,200 men. This draft was retained at Didcot. They camped under canvas on Station Meadow (now Cronshaw Close) and trained there. Later they were billeted on the people of Didcot. The Corn Exchange building (it had ceased trading in *c.* 1899) was converted into a YMCA, and was used by these men and also by those who came later when the arsenal was established.

In October, the National Reserve took over the security of the country's railway system, and locally recruited special constables assumed the battalion's role in guarding the lines. The battalion finally left Didcot on the 11 and 12 November for Sevenoaks. They eventually arrived in France in February 1915.

A story was once current in the town that a high-ranking officer standing on Didcot Station while waiting for a train connection suddenly saw the potential of Didcot as an army base. This is like all the other stories connected with Didcot – completely fictitious. A nice romantic story without any basis in truth.

As for Didcot and the army, the War Office was well aware of the potential of Didcot with its advantageous position in the railway system; and had been so aware since at least 1889, with the establishment of the camp at Churn. It was not until the outbreak of war that transfer of part of the Woolwich Arsenal to Didcot became a matter of urgency. The arsenal's site in London was terribly exposed to shelling by the German Fleet if it should penetrate the Thames Estuary and the river mouth. It became an even wiser move with the advent of the Zepplin raids in early 1916.

The army had long been familiar with Didcot and the area around

Churn camp some years before the First World War. (Mrs Susan Woodall)

it. The Downs at Churn had been used to train volunteers at annual summer camps. Didcot was connected to the Churn camps by the Didcot, Newbury and Southampton Railway. The little station at Churn, which gave access to the Blewbury Downs, had been established for the National Rifle Association. The land for the station had been given by Lord Wantage, who was both a prominent member of the association and a director of the railway company. However, the association preferred Bisley. From 1889 onwards, military camps were held annually each summer. After the death of Lord Wantage in 1901, the army took over the site for permanent use by the military. The Chilton Downs were also used; in the 1890s a large parade, of the Lancers, Scots Greys and the Royal Horse Artillery was held before the Duke of Cambridge. It seems that Didcot was also used for these manoeuvres. The minutes of the RDC record that in 1909, 'an application was received from the Army Authorities for a temporary water connection to be laid on to a field near the [Didcot] Rectory to supply a military camp there in connection with military manoeuvres'. So it can be said with confidence that the War Office had known the Didcot area for the twenty years before 1914. It was only the outbreak of war that determined that the arsenal should be transferred to a new site at Didcot – the need had just not existed before. It may well be that the plans for the removal had been drawn up before 1914, because it was not long before the army was examining the future site in great detail. Mr Cullen remembers his father receiving a telegram in late 1914, instructing him to meet and show a party of high-ranking officers and officials the land on which the arsenal was to be built.

The news soon began to circulate throughout the district in late 1914/early 1915; and in its issue of 23 January 1915, the *Abingdon Herald* reported:

> *Military arrangements*
>
> Many rumours are abroad locally respecting the possibility of Didcot being made a military depot. Officials from the War Office are reported to have visited Didcot several times of late and in conjunction with the Railway Authorities have made exhaustive enquiries. It is rumoured that railway sidings are to be made and barracks built. Whether this is true or not remains to be seen but evidently some scheme is contemplated.

It was only too true. In fact, the *Herald*'s news item was rather premature, because the *Berks and Oxon* had 'scooped' all the other local newspapers in its issue of 10 February 1915, under the heading 'Didcot to be site of new Arsenal'. The story stated that the War Office had decided to supplement the Woolwich Arsenal which was subject to attack both from air and sea, and

> no less than 280 acres of land had been purchased . . . and hundreds of men will be employed in preparing it for the purpose for which it will be put . . . . Didcot is very favourably placed for an Arsenal. There is from the Great Western Railway Station direct communication with the north, south, east and west and it is said that communications will be established with the Thames by cutting a canal from Appleford . . . very extensive operations will be carried out . . . . This will entirely alter the character of the whole neighbourhood and enhance the cost of local labour . . . . Already the Great Western Railway are busily engaged in making new sidings for connection with the main line.

The report was unwittingly prophetic when it continued,

> so it seems that Didcot, which has long been in a semi-dormant state will soon be as busy a place as any part of Berkshire. Hundreds of houses will have to be built, new enterprises and new businesses will come into existence while every bit of land in the neighbourhood will enhance in price.

How right this anonymous correspondent was.

As the local newspapers of the times reported, the War Office in late 1914 or early 1915 had purchased 280 acres of land that lay within the parishes of Didcot, Appleford, Sutton Courtenay, Harwell and Milton. The major farm was Durnells Farm in Sutton Courtenay. The army barracks were to be sited within Didcot and the ordnance depot on the north side of the railway, mainly in Sutton Courtenay and Milton.

After this length of time, it is not known how the villagers of Old Didcot or the railway families of Northbourne reacted to the arrival of the army in 1915. Presumably attitudes, especially in Old Didcot, varied on how people benefited from its presence. To a certain extent any adverse reaction would have been influenced by the almost universal patriotism of those early war years. Also the move to Didcot was so unexpected. But later resentment did become widespread as the barracks and the depot grew in size.

The army often acted arbitrarily, excusing its behaviour with a 'don't you know there's a war on' attitude. The resentment was due to a number of reasons. By the end of the war, there was a large workforce, both military and civilian, employed at the depot, causing difficulties in several ways. Firstly, a housing famine was created. The Joint Workers Committee pointed out, 'that there is an urgent need for increasing housing accommodation at Didcot and that the District Council should take steps to improve the same as soon as the war is over'. A survey of November 1917 found that there was an urgent need for housing. The water supply was also a problem. The army, in June 1916, gave an estimate to the council that it would need 45,000 gallons per week, but it was soon found that they were in reality using 56,000 gallons. Consequently, the civilian population of Didcot and Northbourne were severely deprived of water during the daylight hours; the council was soon beset by vociferous complaints from irate local ratepayers. The situation did not improve because the army's water demands grew even greater. Disposal of sewage was another problem. With the help of the army, a loan was secured, and the sewage works extended.

But many in the village soon realized that there were advantages to be found. Food and spare clothing could be had at the cookhouse at the weekends by those who were not too proud to beg; and there were other products. 'Bodger' Smith of Smiths Farm used human sewage from the barracks to fertilize his fields, which lay to the west of the village. The late Walter Davies remembers that the smell, all pervading, would envelop the village when the wind was in the west, as it usually was.

But one thing is clear: the villagers and the railway families were generally unaware of the War Office's plans for Didcot and the surrounding parishes. Though they were not a secret. Newspaper reports had appeared in early 1915 detailing those plans. So when the first huts were erected in April 1915, it came as a great surprise, and probably it did not register even then how large the depot was going to be, or how large the number of troops and civilians who would be working and living almost on top of them. Even the army had to modify and enlarge its plans for Didcot as the war went on and on in its ferocity, and in its insatiable demands for munitions.

Certainly, Mr Cullen did not know at the time, and neither, it seems, did his mother. It would have been their sole topic of conversation and that of the community at large had the news been commonplace, but it was not. This is not so surprising as it might appear. In those days, the communication of news was slow and erratic, before the era of radio and television. Newspapers were bought only by those who could afford them – even with a branch of W.H. Smith near the station. News for Didcot came mainly from the railway station with its telegraph and telephone. Another source of news for the villagers was the Queen's Arms, the village pub.

For Walter Davies, the army's arrival in Didcot was a tragedy of the first order, a tragedy which for him reverberated down throughout the remainder of his life. The Old Didcot that he knew, where he had spent his childhood, was a close knit, warm community, where everyone was known, and where there was always a helping hand for those who needed it. The village was set in unspoilt countryside, which intensive farming had yet to spoil, that teamed with wildlife – insects, the humble cricket, wild flowers galore and birds of every description.

The army started the process that destroyed this tranquillity, its isolation and the innocence of its people. Before 1914, the rural population was happy with its poverty-stricken lot. Mr Davies wrote that, 'all was tranquillity and peace of mind, when people were satisfied with their lot'. But the unceasing burden of the war years – far heavier than 1939–45 – wore down workers' spirits and even happy-go-lucky and previously contented youngsters began to feel that they were being overworked, exploited and underpaid. The contentment of the pre-1914 era as expressed by Mr Davies was effectively destroyed during the Great War.

To a certain extent, he, in old age, was looking back with increased nostalgia to his lost childhood, and to a world that had gone for ever, one that had disappeared sixty or seventy years ago. The loss of this world was summed up for him in the destruction by the army of the meadows north of the railway where the depot was sited (now the power station site), which he in his childhood called the 'Happy Lands'. Everyone else saw them as boggy meadows of little value. But he described them thus:

> it [the depot] was sited on fields that we knew as the 'Happy Lands'. I remember these as especially beautiful fields. And it still saddens me to think what has been lost in the name of progress. There were clear flowing streams where I used to catch bull-heads, and have my annual bath, which ran through quiet meadows that slumbered undisturbed throughout the year, except at haymaking and harvest times. The only noise was that of the ploughman (no noisy tractors or harvesters), and, of course, always the constant song of birds.

Though poor, Mr Davies did have a happy childhood.

He was one of the few eyewitnesses to those years; and the only one to have written down his memories of 1914. He remembered the arrival of the army:

> That winter, 1914–15, was very mild, not a lot of snow but being short handed on the farm [that of Dennis Napper's] there was always plenty to do. . . . The beginnings of the Ordnance Depot began about the time of haymaking in 1915, when we saw several men in Happy Lands. They were the fields on the other side of the railway, opposite Cow Meadow, down the Weygrounds. They were walking around with measuring tapes, sticking marking poles in the ground, and some men were using surveying instruments. . . . Then during the same month, May 1915, a week or

The Barracks in 1915. *(Don Farnborough)*

two later, a large number of pre-fabricated huts were erected on the allotments that used to be on the west side of Vauxhall Lane, opposite the Rectory. They looked like Army huts as there was a notice that had 'W.D.' painted on it. This was fixed to the gate of the allotments. The men who had allotments there were taking all their stuff, plants, produce and sheds, away. We asked one of these men what the huts were for. He told us that they were for the soldiers who was going to live there, and that the Army were going to build over the railway bridge somewhere. Then we remembered the men who we had seen earlier that month. Soon afterwards, the soldiers arrived and began occupying the huts. Their armbands told us that they were 'labour' and 'pioneers'.

To add to this news, Dad told us what the railwaymen had told him during one of his visits to the Queens Arms. Trains carrying equipment, stores, building supplies, etc., were coming in to the sidings; it was all owned by the Army. They were just waiting for another railway line to be laid down by the side of the Copse, and into the fields beyond

Time went on, and work began on the Depot. Later that winter, we were mole spreading in Cow Meadow, and over the other side of the railway, in our 'Happy Lands', we saw hundreds of men at work. They were up to their eyes in mud, cutting down trees, pulling up hedges and filling in ditches. There were horses and carts all over the place, all engaged in carrying away the debris. The noise, at least to us, was deafening, it was bedlam over there, the peace and quiet that had existed for centuries was being brutally shattered. . . .

The men were still frantically busy in the 'Happy Lands'; though that name was hardly applicable any more. There were hundreds out there busy with showels and all types of machines digging what looked like foundations for buildings. Sadly we were now finished with those fields by the look of things. . . .

The arrival of the Army and the troops had obviously been seen by some as a means of making money. A man named Barber had been busy. He built a small hut at the end of Vauxhall Railway Bridge, from which he sold tobacco, cigarettes, sweets, tea and food. . . . The hut was always open, seven days a week, and it was always busy for there was usually someone being served whenever you passed. I walked down there on a Sunday, and a lot of soldiers were all gathered around the hut, buying tobacco and drinking tea. Also standing there were about twenty very tall policemen, formed up in two ranks, all about to be marched off. They all wore helmets and armbands. I was told that they had come from London; and as I looked on they marched away towards the Copse, over the bridge, and beyond to the site of the works. The site was off-limits to us villagers, it was guarded by those policemen who wouldn't let anyone near. But we could see all we wanted from Cow Meadow, though we wern't that interested.

All the local farmers benefited, for the Provender Stores which provided hay and grain for railway horses, had to go on nightshift to keep pace with the demands made by the Army to feed the many hundreds of horses they were using on the Depot sit. . . .

The Depot was gradually taking place. Long sheds sprang up seemingly overnight. Trains loaded with everything you could imagine were coming from all over the country to Didcot, through the station, and into the Depot. There were a constant stream of trains. We could hear them all the time. We heard that they were taking guns, tents, mule carts and everything the Army required. We were definitely on the map at last.

At Milton there were gangs of chinese labourers living in huts which we used to call China Town. This part of the depot belonged to the Royal Flying Corps; aeroplanes were getting as common as were motor cars; they were no longer the frightening things that we used to think. The passenger station was always crowded with soldiers coming and going on leave or back to France.

Walter Davies' memoirs are invaluable as a source of oral history, which, unusually, he wrote down, and which also reflect the attitudes of the villagers at that time, though to a certain extent it must be said that his memories were tainted by modern environmentalist views, which he could not have held at the time. If he did have views and opinions – he was 14 at the time – it is more likely he would share those of his elders: resentment at the intrusion of the army into their rural isolation. This was precisely their attitude towards the railwaymen. Mr Davies still felt that way – resentment towards Northbourne and the railwaymen as late as the 1970s. His timescales are slightly out; and the latter part of the excerpt relates to 1916 onwards.

Not only were there soldiers at the depot, Didcot was also designated as an area where wounded soldiers were to be treated. The

During the First World War the Rectory was used for troop convalescence. Here nurses and wounded soldiers play musical chairs.

two day schools in Northbourne and Old Didcot were scheduled in August 1914 to be hospitals, though they were never used as such. The Rector of All Saints, the Revd John Brown and Mrs Brown did care for soldiers who were recuperating before returning to France.

Mr Davies was the only observer to note the presence at Didcot of the London policemen in charge of security at the depot, and more important the establishment of Jackson's shop at the side of the Foxhall Railway Bridge, in 1915.

Before the building of the depot, the area of farmland, as Mr Davies described it, was quite beautiful, and not the dismal industrial landscape that prevails today, stretching away on all sides beyond the two railway bridges. Before the enclosures of 1800–1, this was Sutton Courtenay's common lands, known as 'Sutton Moor', and was still known as such during the nineteenth century. Hard to believe that the present-day site of Didcot power station was once regarded as a 'desolate and unfrequented place', where, as *Jackson's Oxford Journal* reported in November 1838, 'a Mr F. Adams of Sutton Courtenay was attacked by two villains'.

The main farm to be created out of that enclosure was Durnells Farm; and it was this farm that was the main property to be acquired by the army in 1914. The present-day Basil Hill Road (named after a high-ranking officer at the depot) before 1914 was a tree-lined country lane – if not a track – which gave access to the Durnell farmhouse. The farmhouse has gone: its former site is now covered by the power station.

9

Didcot Arsenal and Depot, 1915–1918

The sequence of events in early 1915 was roughly as Mr Davies remembered them, though his was a largely unfocused view. He could see but did not know what was actually happening.

Work began in late March, and on both sides of the railway. Huts to accommodate '300 men' were erected in Foxhall Road, and there was feverish activity on the other side of the line. Initially the camp was to be quite a modest affair but the progress of the war changed all that. The biggest problem experienced by the army in those early war years was the lack of man-power. Not only was the depot located in an area of thinly populated and scattered villages, but much of the existing man-power had already enlisted. Such was the shortage of labour at the end of 1915 that the unit almost ceased to exist.

However, work did begin in Mr Davies' 'Happy Lands'. A contemporary new item appeared in the *Berks and Oxon Advertizer* for 15 April 1915, which is given here in an edited form:

The Didcot Arsenal

> The work of constructing the new Arsenal at Didcot is in full swing, and a recent visit gave some idea but a very faint one, of the magnitude of the undertaking. All the hedges that separated the different meadows have been cut down, most of the timber has been felled, and several lines of railway have been laid. The whole site is intersected with railways. The workmen were engaged removing turf to prepare for the erection of buildings.

The entrance to the barracks just after the First World War.

A great number of sites were marked out for this purpose. In some places concrete has already been laid. On the line connecting with and alongside the Great Western Railway, platforms for the receipt of materials had already been completed, and are in use. Thousands of tons of plant and material had already been delivered there. Huge locomotives were at work drawing this material to the different locations where it was required, and a great number of workmen were busy (although it was Bank Holiday) in carrying out the directions of those in charge. For considerably more than a mile the ground is covered with men, materials and locomotives. What seems to be intended for a waterway in connection with the Thames at Appleford, has been commenced and huge amounts of earth have been excavated in the process. Notices were posted in Lord Kitchener's name asking for the earnest co-operation of the men in facilitating the work, and it was evidently working, for every man was industriously and methodically plodding on. . . . Whole rows of huts are being erected on the high ground on the south side of the railway for the temporary housing of work people and the navvies are finding accommodation in Didcot and the neighbouring villages.

> That a great number of houses will be required for the workers is certain. Although the Arsenal will doubtless benefit the district financially, one could not but regret that this fine tract of land is henceforth given up for the purpose of manufacturing shot and shell and other implements of destruction.

The strangest thing about this report, other than some feeling that there is an element of exaggeration, is the proposed construction of a canal. This had been mentioned before in an earlier report from the *Berks and Oxon Advertizer*. It seems quite illogical. A canal would take a year or more to construct at great expense and need a large labour-force, which simply was not available at that time. The workforce that this correspondent saw came from outside, it certainly did not originate locally.

It is very curious, because the information must have been given to him by someone at the time. But no mention is made of a canal in any other record – such as the army's informal history of the depot and arsenal, which incidentally states, 'in its original concept the depot was to consist of twenty-eight sheds'. In those circumstances, the construction of a canal seems somewhat excessive, especially when the railway was at hand.

The depot was formally opened by Captain George Payne, with fifteen officers and men on 15 June 1915. In his letter to S. Allen Warner, of November 1957, he described the depot as he saw it on that first day:

> We arrived on the 15 June 1915, and after billeting my men, I took a reccee and my first view. I did not go to the top of the Provender Store, but onto a narrow and very inadequate little bridge just beyond. What I saw was firstly a field with a few huts under construction, on the site of the present site of Vauxhall Barracks, then from the little bridge I saw a narrow dirt track (the present Basil Hill Road) leading alongside the copse, turning right and ending at Durnells Farm. A large acreage of fruit trees on the right and the rest of the Depot site of growing wheat. On my left the A to D sheds were in course of erection. Traffic sheds too were in the skeleton stage, and the GWR were laying the railway system into the depot.

He then began accepting munitions into the depot. In July, the main body of men arrived, 53 Coy. AOC, which had been formed

A group of servicemen at the depot.

that month, 168 men of all ranks, under Captain Stanborough. The depot was under the overall command of Colonel C. Purchas, Chief Ordnance Officer, Didcot.

The role of the depot, as the army stated, was 'to receive, store, and issue a great deal of general stores required to support the British and Commonwealth Armies all over the World'; and soon after his arrival Captain Payne did just that – take delivery of stores. Later he established a magazine area, over which he had charge (Captain Payne was a gunnery officer), and during the rest of the war, tons and tons of small-arms ammunition was received and sent on to France and other theatres of war.

Strange as it may seem, the number of men was just inadequate to transfer the sheer volume of materials and munitions that were arriving every day, from the railway trucks into the sheds. Consequently, there was an equally long delay in shipping them out to the war fronts.

As Captain Payne wrote, 'the stores starting to come in from the various factories and soon we turned those wheat acres into a seething mass of MUD, MUD, MUD and water. Never did I see such a wet and dismal situation, not a road or the resemblance of one.' He went on to record his appreciation of the Great Western Railway, 'do not forget the railway system in the Depot. Had it not been for the efficient services of the railway, Didcot Depot would never have been finished. Without the railway we should all have sunk in the mud.'

The situation was becoming critical, with stores and other materials piling up, railway trucks waiting to be unloaded, when Colonel Purchas had the brilliant idea of appealing to the university authorities at Oxford for help. He described his problems in a letter to Lord Desborough of the Central Association of Volunteer Training Corps, that 'about a month ago [i.e. October 1915] I found it was becoming impossible with the force of the Army Ordnance Corps here to receive all the supplies coming in from all sources, and to issue them promptly. At my wits' end I went to Oxford . . .'. At Oxford, he saw the commanding officers of the Oxford Volunteer Regiment, and of the 1st and 2nd Battalion. They promised all help possible with the men of the VT Corps, the OT Corps and the Ordnance Corps. But no civilians should be involved. Colonel Purchas also saw the Vice-Chancellor, and he undertook to do what he could that members of the university should join and be available.

The response was magnificent. The result of his appeal was two-fold. Not only did he get the help needed, but membership of the Volunteer Corps increased dramatically, because to assist at Didcot meant being a member of the corps. Ultimately, as a result of helping at Didcot, many joined the university OT Corps; the Berkshire VT Corps increased in numbers, and there were many enlistments into the regular army from the VT Corps. He was able to report with some pride that

> supplies to our troops overseas from Didcot have been made without any delay . . . [and this] result would not have been attained without the help from the O.T.C. Bodies of the V.T. Corps have come to help us, especially on Sundays, from Oxford, Maidenhead, Taplow, Banbury and also from Reading, where over 800 men gave their services. Berkshire having heard of the help given by Oxford, and being equally anxious to help the country in this crisis. Offers of help have also come from the V.T.C. in Bucks and other counties. The magnitude of the voluntary aid thus given is shown by the fact that the number of truck loads dealt with on Sunday, October 24, was 98, on Sunday, October 31, 63 and on Sunday, November 11, 209. The contents of those unloaded were properly disposed of and stacked away, besides very much other work inside the store houses, including packing, painting, etc.

The volunteers at Oxford University included heads of houses, graduates and undergraduates, with many dons, and the Principal of Mansfield, the Vice-Principal of St Edmund's, the Regius Professor of Greek, Prince George of Teck. Public schoolboys from Eton and Radley came on several occasions. Among the Eton group was Prince Henry, later Duke of Gloucester. But the mass of volunteers came from the civilian population, who had enrolled in the volunteers corps, from all over Oxfordshire and Berkshire. As another contributor to *The Times* pointed out in a letter, the actual contribution from Oxford University was quite small in comparison.

The volunteers increased in numbers week by week, so that by the middle of November the scale of activity at Didcot became so great that it came to the notice of *The Times*, when an article describing the scene appeared on Monday 15th – and was probably the first time such an item had appeared about Didcot in that august newspaper. Thus over the nation's breakfast tables Didcot became famous for a brief moment, and was held up as an example to all when the use of volunteers at other establishments was suggested and acted upon. *The Times* article set the scene; and it is from this report that the wildly inaccurate figure of 3,000 men having attended on one Sunday, 7 November, came, when the correct number was about 900. The article, appearing under the headline 'Zeal at Didcot: Dons among the workers. Busy Sunday scenes', continued:

> Didcot Junction is the last place in the world where you would expect anything to begin. It consists of a inexpressively dreary railway station. . . . In the flat and somewhat marshy meadows that surround this tangle of railway lines the War Office decided some months ago to create a store. Some hundreds of acres were secured, contractors were appointed to erect some miles of shed, and here in due course were sent some officers and about 80 men. The men set to work with a will. They tugged and lifted and hauled and pushed until they were exhausted, and then they set to work again. But lines of trucks grew longer and the long sheds were filled with depressing slowness. Depression would have settled on this band of heroic soldiers had not an inspiration come to Colonel Purchas. He appealed to the Authorities at Oxford University for help. The training Corps offered to come in a body the following Saturday, and they were joined by a party of Dons and Undergraduates, making a force of between 300 and 400 volunteers.

> The work of shunting and unloading went cheerfully foward all that day and the next. Here might be seen a learned professor painting a bucket, whilst a renowned historian carried plates. All the week small parties of Dons or Oxford citizens came over to carry on the work, and at the following week-end, the Oxford contingent, 400 strong, found themselves reinforced by about 300 helpers from the neighbouring villages. The volunteers had brought their band, which played them to and from their labours.
>
> Meanwhile the news spread through the countryside that there was urgent work to be done at Didcot. One Sunday, instead of 300 helpers, nearly 3000 came over from Oxford, Witney, Banbury, Thame, Reading, Maidenhead, Henley, Windsor, Goring and Streatley, Bicester and Chipping Norton. Mr Mason, M.P., as he stated in the House of Commons on Wednesday, took over a large contingent from Windsor, and Lord Desborough, came over and took command. So well did this amateur army work under the direction of the small Regular Force that hundreds of trucks were unloaded and the line cleared.
>
> Yesterday the volunteers numbered more than 2000, drawn from all parts of Oxfordshire and the surrounding counties and even from Northampton. Five bands played the workers to their tasks. A large number were set to unload tons of nails. Others unloaded oil and similar articles.
>
> The limit of enthusiasm has not yet been reached, and offers of help continue to come in. Next Thursday 700 members of the Eton O.T.C. under Dr Lyttelton, are to come down to Didcot. The Radley School O.T.C. has volunteered to paint buckets on three days in the week, and the first offer of service from London has been received, the workers in this case being members of the Kensington Volunteer Regiment.

Volunteers still continued to attend the fledgling depot throughout the remainder of 1915 and into early 1916. Among the many volunteer groups were boys from the Kingston Industrial School. Further help was given, almost constantly, by a party of ladies, numbering from sixteen to twenty, who came in daily, excepting Saturdays and Sundays, and for nearly eighteen months.

Quoting from an almost contemporary and anonymous letter of *c*. 1920, the writer stated that

> after this [the volunteer period] the labour question improved and

Eton boys unloading railway trucks, late in 1915.

during June 1917, 1000 men and 431 women and by the middle of July, 1547 men and 552 women were employed. In August 1918, the number of employees reached 1560 men and 756 women, the number fluctuated considerably from then up to the signing of the Armistice. It was also found, as the Depot grew, that the number of R.A.O.C., would prove insufficient, and towards the end of 1917, two labour companies, each of 500 men, were told off definitely for duty at Didcot.

In total there were 1,900 troops of all ranks stationed at Didcot by the end of 1918; these in addition to the large civilian force employed at the depot.

The sheer volume of war materials arriving every day was such that a large labour-force was needed not only to unload but to reload trucks again for dispatch to the war front. In 1916, 7,080 railway trucks were unloaded; in 1917, 9,486; and in 1918, 9,952. The largest number handled in one month was 1,103, in April 1918.

The depot rapidly increased in size: from the original concept of twenty-eight sheds to, by the end of the war, forty-five sheds, with additional workshops, and twenty magazine buildings. A seven-line marshalling yard was built with off-sets to feed the store sheds. Internal roads were also built. In all, by the end of 1918, the depot had been extended to cover 1.5 million sq ft of covered accommodation with 30 miles of railway tracks and sidings. The function of the depot during the Great War was to supply 'vote 8' or general stores and small arms ammunition, and these were supplied to the many theatres of war.

The importance of the railway in the development of the depot cannot be over-emphasized. Captain Payne had given the Great Western full credit for their help in those early days. To repeat his remarks, 'Had it not been for the efficient services of the railway, Didcot Depot would never have been finished. Without the railway, we should all have sunk in the mud.'

As can be imagined, the overall effect on Didcot, especially the old village, was traumatic, even if this was cumulative as the depot grew in size from its early beginnings in 1915 to the large complex of 1918, its workforce finally reaching nearly 4,000 by the end of the war.

It's hard for us today to appreciate how isolated this area was before the Great War, where news was slow in coming, where people were weeks behind events. As the army appreciated, it was an area 'of thinly populated and scattered villages', where labour was just not available, hence the rush of volunteers at the end of 1915.

The villagers were very happy in their isolation, resenting deeply the presence of outsiders – witness their long-held animosity towards Northbourne and its inhabitants. The cultural impact must have been tremendous as these 4,000 workers were virtually encamped right on their doorstep and also living in their midst. Not only did these workers have different values, they also brought crime to Didcot. Before the Great War, the squire and parson were the rulers and the arbiters of behaviour, but no longer. The old standards were disappearing fast. After 1918, Old Didcot was never to be the same again.

The army, in its own insensitive way, also tended to alienate the villagers by its arbitrary behaviour. In June 1918, the parish council wrote to the district council asking what steps they should take to 'maintain their right to use the occupation Road leading from the main Wantage Road to the village'. Presumably, the army had

Another group outside the old Corn Exchange which by that time had been converted into a YMCA. A play, appropriately entitled The soldier's rendezvous, *is being staged.*

stopped the villagers using the upper part of Foxhall Road. The district council also had a similar complaint: a big pile of stones had been left at the junction of Foxhall Road–Wantage Road for road repairs. The army took the lot without asking if they could, to be used to build a platform for a searchlight.

It was no more easy for the newcomers – they were only too aware of this resentment. Conditions for these former city dwellers were poor. Housing was virtually unobtainable. As mentioned earlier, the Workers' Joint Committee had pointed out in March 1917, that there was an urgent need for housing to be provided after the war.

Mrs Watson, in her letter of 1951, summed it up, when she wrote of the conditions here when she and her husband arrived at Didcot in 1915:

> We came here on 1st April 1915, and found the place almost unbearable: but we had to live here . . . . Parish Councillors who could not write their own names, who opposed everything these few railwaymen wanted to do . . . . No council houses, no lighting, no electricity, no gas, no hot and cold water, no hospital, no resident doctor, no nurse, no chemist shop. These few people (including myself) were positively hated by these few inhabitants.

Although Mrs Watson was a railwayman's wife, her experience must have been shared by many, including the newcomers to the depot.

But the depot did confer benefits on Didcot and the area, such as jobs. It also gave Didcot the western half of Station Road. Before 1917, Station Road ended at the station, at the western end of the large roundabout fronting the station – or Station Approach.

The army needing a more direct route from the depot to the station – the earlier way had been through the village, via Lydalls Lane – laid down the upper part of Station Road about April 1917. The military had done what the RDC had wanted to do years before but had been unable to justify the expense at that time.

The end of the war had left the Wallingford Rural District Council with all the problems, such as inadequate housing and poor water supplies, that the army had created. By solving them, the local authority was to start the next phase in the development and expansion of Didcot.

Appendix 1

Original building dates and owners of Northbourne's houses and cottages

For almost all the houses and cottages below, the building dates and names of original owners given are correct; where there is an element of doubt, the symbol [?] indicates that the details are speculative.

Road or street	Original owner	Building date
Bourne Street		
2–12	G.E. Hobbs	1884
16	Revd B.J. Summersby	1887
Broadway		
Marsh Cottages	George Napper	1863
25–7 (demolished)	Mrs Caroline Robbins	*c.* 1895
29–41	George Evans	1886
43 (shop)	John Pryor	1890
45–7	John Lay	1869
49–55	John Lay	1869
57–9	Thomas Andrews	1872–3
61	Thomas Andrews	1879
63–5	Stephen Dixon	1879
67–71	Stephen Dixon	1877
73–9	Mrs Lightfoot	1871
81–3	R.J. Wood	1869

93 Newtown Cottage (demolished)	Henry Wright	1869
95–101	G.C. Hobbs	1883
105–7	Warner West	1867–8
109–11 (demolished)	Warner West	1867–8
113–15 (demolished)	Warner West	1867–8
117–21	James Banwell	1874
123 Hope Cottage	Robert Haines	1871
125 Highfield House [now Barclays Bank]	George Drewe	1873

Church Street

2–16	Stephen Dixon	1870–3
38–40	R.J. Wood	1873
42–4	R.J. Wood	1873
46–50	Thomas Faulkner	1869
7–29	Stephen Dixon	1870–3
35	Jabez Martin	1874
37–9	James Townsend	1879
41–3	James Tyrrell	1872
45–7	Elizabeth Townsend	1870
49–55	Thomas Faulkner	1903
57–9	James Lintern	1883

Until quite recently, nos 38–40 were front-parlour shops: no. 38 was Gays, the hairdresser, and no. 40, was a fried fish shop. In the late nineteenth century, no. 35 was also a shop, a cordwainers.

East Street

3–5	Mrs Sidery	1879 [?]
9–11	Fred Keep	1880 [?]
13–15	[not known]	
17–19	James Lavell	1882
23–5	Revd B.J. Summersby	1881 [?]
12	[not known]	early 1900s
14	John Irving	1882
16	John Irving	1882
18	[not known]	

20	Fred Keep	1881
22–4	James Walters	1881–2

Hagbourne Road

4–10	Stephen Dixon	1870
12–14	James Pether	1869
16–18	[not known]	1906
26 The Sprat	Messrs Pittman	1879–80
28 Carey Cottage	Fred Keep	1873

[Carey Cottage was lived in for a long period by the Pughs, a well-known Northbourne family. They were there as late as the 1920s.]

High Street

1–7 (demolished)	E.L. Shepherd	1870
9 (Dales)	Richard Edwards	1890
33–5	Stephen Cox	1886
2	School committee	*c.* 1894
4–16	Stephen Dixon	*c.* 1880–3
18 (shop)	Stephen Dixon	1880

Mereland Road

3	John Brewer	1873
5–7 Monckton House	James Banwell	1874
9–13 The Trinity	George Drewe	1880

Wessex Road

8–6	[not known]	*c.* 1901
14	[not known]	early 1890s [?]
16–18	[not known]	early 1890s [?]
20	Henry Griffin	1898
22–6	Fred Belcher	1882
28–32	John Burridge	*c.* 1879
34–6 [26 High Street]	Mr Challenor	*c.* 1892
40–2	Stephen Cox	1891
58–60	Wilks and Whitfield	*c.* 1890

Appendix 2

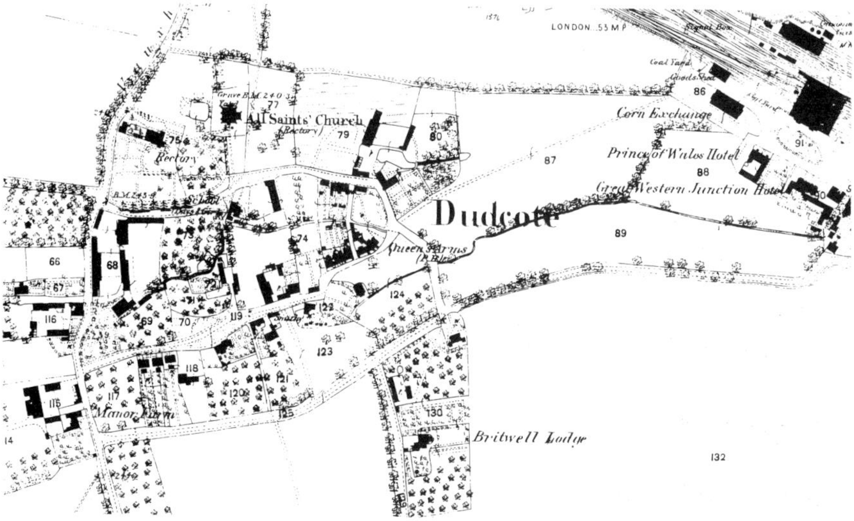

Above *Didcot village and station in 1876;* below *Old Didcot and Northbourne, 1900.*

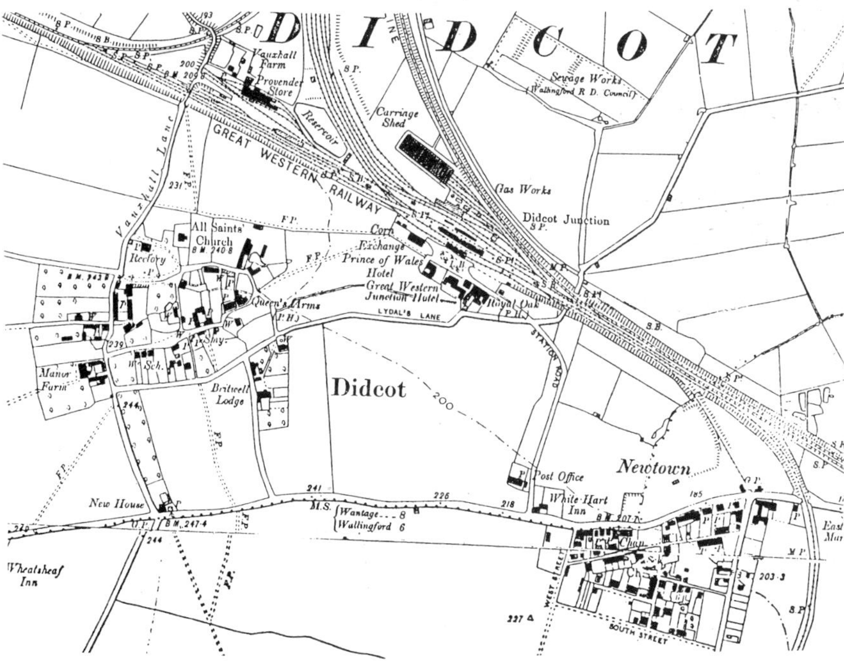

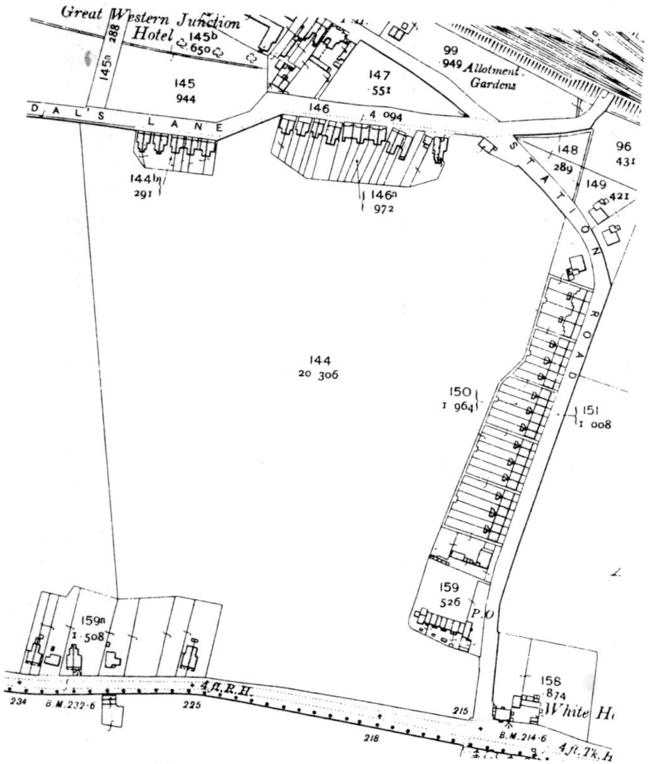

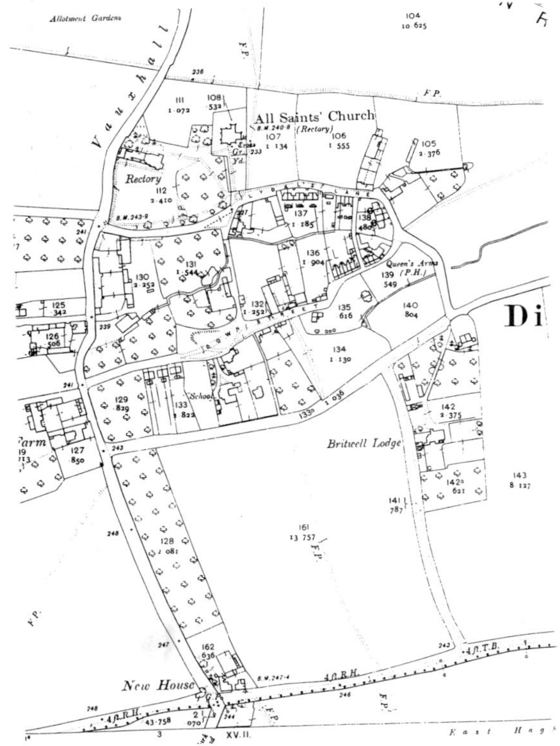

Left *Spiral development along Wallingford Road, Station Road and lower Lydalls Road in 1912;* right *Didcot village, 1912.*

Sources

Books

Place of publication given only if outside London.

Gibbs, G.H., *Birth of the Great Wetern Railway: Diary of G.H. Gibbs*, ed. Jack Simmons, Bath, Adams & Dart, 1971.
Havinden, M.A., *Estate Village, a Study of the Berkshire Villages of Ardington and Lockinge*, 1966.
Hodgkinson, Albert The King's Own TF in the European War, 1914–12918 [1–Stn Batallion, the King's Own (Royal Lancashire Regiment)], Lewes, Lewes Press, 1921.
MacDermot, E.T., *History of the GWR*, 3 vols; rev. C.R. Clinker, Ian Allan, 1982.
Pawson, Eric, *Transport and Economy: Turnpike Roads of the 18th century*, Academic Press, 1977.
Simmons, Ernest J., *Memoirs of a Stationmaster (1879)*, ed. Jack Simmons, Bath, Adams & Dart, 1974.
Waters, Laurence, *Didcot Junction and Railway Centre*, Ian Allan, 1989.

Census returns

Didcot, 1841–81
Northbourne, 1881

Deeds

Northbourne house deeds, several of which were loaned to the author. The earliest ones give a recital of Stephen Dixon's transactions with his mortgagors

Documents and manuscripts

All Saints Church, Didcot Churchwardens' Accounts, 1754–1870
Davies, Walter [Memoirs], 1977
Didcot Parish Council: minutes; Enclosure Award
East Hagbourne Parish Council: minutes
Evans, Roger, 'Some aspects of the impact of the Railway on 19th Century Didcot', n.d.
St Peter's Church, Northbourne: notes
Tame, Miss E.M., letters to the author
Wallingford Board of Guardians: ratebooks, 1863–97
Wallingford Sanitary/Rural District Council: minutes, 1878–1918
War Office: unofficial history of the arsenal/depot at Didcot [typescript]
Warner, S. Allen: chronological notes, 1720–1952; newspaper articles, 1950–52

Maps

Ordnance Survey 25 in series: 1st edn. 1874; 2nd edn. 1899; 3rd edn. 1912

Newspapers

Berks and Oxon Advertizer
Great Western Magazine
Jackson's Oxford Journal
Reading Mercury
The Star
The Times

Obituaries: *Didcot Advertizer*

McFarlane, George, November 1950
Robert Rich, January 1937

Trade Directories

Billings
Kelly's
Post Office, 1847–1903

Index